Test Your Vocabulary for FCE

Rawdon Wyatt

... Education Limited
... urgh Gate
... arlow
Essex CM20 2JE, England
and Associated Companies throughout the world.

ISBN 0 582 45175 2

This edition published 2002
Text copyright © Rawdon Wyatt 2002

Designed and typeset by Pantek Arts Ltd, Maidstone, Kent
Test Your format devised by Peter Watcyn-Jones
Illustrations by Martin Fish, Vince Silcock and Ross Thomson
Printed in Italy by Rotolito Lombarda

Acknowledgements
The author would like to thank the following:
The students at St. Clare's, Oxford, for piloting these tests and for providing invaluable feedback. Jan Kelly and Mark Searle, teachers extraordinaire at St. Clare's, Oxford, for their many useful comments and suggestions. Claire de Gruchy, for her inexhaustible support, encouragement and supplies of grinning grunters. Judith Greet, for editing the whole thing and suggesting useful changes. Helen Parker, Jane Durkin and all at Penguin Longman.

Published by Pearson Education Limited in association with Penguin Books Ltd, both companies being subsidiaries of Pearson plc.

For a complete list of the titles available from Penguin English please visit our website at www.penguinenglish.com, or write to your local Pearson Education office or to: Marketing Department, Penguin Longman Publishing, 80 Strand, London WC2R 0RL.

Contents

To the student

If you are going to take the Cambridge First Certificate exam, you will find the tests in this book very helpful. They will help you practise a lot of the vocabulary that you might need to use in the Writing, Speaking or Use of English papers, or that you might come across in the Reading or Listening papers. Many of the tests also have useful information on how you might be expected to use the vocabulary in the exam.

There are three sections in the book:

- Section 1 deals with general vocabulary items that may be relevant in the exam as a whole.

- Section 2 deals with particular topics that are very common in the exam, and which you may have to write or speak about.

- Section 3 deals with particular tasks in the exam, such as those in the Speaking Test and Writing Paper, and provides you with useful words and expressions.

There is a key at the back of the book so that you can check your answers.

You should *not* try to work through every test in this book. Instead, you should choose vocabulary areas that you are not familiar with, or areas that you are particularly interested in.

Don't forget to keep a record of new vocabulary items that you come across, and try to use these items as much as possible before the exam.

This book tests most of the vocabulary you will need to know for the exam, but don't forget that you can learn new words and expressions by reading as much as possible from a variety of different sources. If you have access to English-language magazines, newspapers and books, you should try to use these to develop your vocabulary.

When you use this book, you will find that a good dictionary will help you. You should choose a dictionary that gives you examples of words in a sentence, so that you can see how words work with other words. The *Longman Active Study Dictionary* is ideal for your level.

If you want to improve your grammar as well as your vocabulary, you might like to use the Penguin book which accompanies this one. It's called *Test Your Grammar and Usage for FCE*.

Good luck in the exam!

Rawdon Wyatt

1 Likes and dislikes

Rearrange the letters in bold to form words or expressions related to likes and dislikes. There is an example at the beginning (0).

0 I'm **eatnosispa batou** fast cars, and have
always wanted a Ferrari. _passionate about_

Likes

1 My sister's boyfriend is so handsome.
I really **nafyc** him. _____

2 My mother is so kind and gentle. I **earod** her. _____

3 My brother is one of the best people in
the world. I absolutely **horswip** him. _____

4 I always **kolo drawrof ot** the summer holidays. _____

5 Sometimes I **goln orf** a bit of peace and quiet. _____

6 I have always been **ratactetd ot** my best
friend's sister. _____

7 I'm quite **donf fo** Chinese food. _____

8 My brother and I are both **enek no** sailing
and go every weekend. _____

Dislikes

1 I will eat almost anything, but I really
thae seafood. _____

2 I'm afraid I **heatlo** people who interrupt
when I'm speaking. _____

3 I **setted** people who tell lies. _____

4 My mother **tanc' dants** listening to loud
music. _____

5 And my father **nact' aerb** being in the
same room as somebody who is smoking. _____

6 The smell of cooking meat really **pleser** me. _____

7 His dirty habits **stugsid** her. _____

8 People who are cruel to animals **tolerv** me. _____

2 Actions

A Put these actions into the appropriate box, depending on which part of the body does them. Some of them can belong in more than one box. There is an example in each box.

> ~~beckon~~ ~~blink~~ ~~cough~~ ~~crawl~~ creep cross dash
> flex frown gaze glance glare glimpse grab groan
> grope hiccup jump laugh leap limp march mutter
> nudge pant pat peep peer point puff punch rub
> scream shout sigh slap slip snap snarl sneeze
> sniff snore squeeze stagger stammer stare stretch
> stroke stroll tap throw trip trudge wander watch
> wave whisper wink wipe yawn yell

Things we do with our arms and hands	Things we do with our mouth and nose
beckon	*cough*
Things we do with our feet and legs	**Things we do with our eyes**
crawl	*blink*

B Complete these sentences with the most appropriate word from the opposite page. You will need to change most of the forms. There is an example at the beginning (0).

0 I saw the bus approaching and _____ *dashed* _____ for the bus stop.

1 She _____ through the smoke-filled room on her hands and knees.

2 He _____ in terror when he saw the snake.

3 We spent most of the morning _____ with difficulty through the thick snow.

4 I _____ a sudden movement out of the corner of my eye.

5 Brian was _____ us to join him.

6 She _____ violently. 'Bless you', I said.

7 I watched the cat slowly _____ towards the unsuspecting bird.

8 I asked her why she was _____ , and she told me she didn't understand the homework.

9 The last time I saw her, she was _____ goodbye to me from the beach.

10 She _____ all night and kept me awake.

11 The audience were _____ their feet in time to the music.

12 They _____ at me angrily, not saying a word.

13 I _____ her with my elbow and told her to be quiet.

14 Sally _____ with relief when she eventually saw him.

In the exam ...
You are often asked to write a story in Part 2 of the Writing Paper. If you write a story, you many find some of the words in this test useful, and they will help to make your writing more interesting.

3 Comparison and contrast

Complete these sentences with the most appropriate word or expression.
There is an example at the beginning (0).

0 British people and people in my country have a lot _____ .

(A) in common   **B** in similar   **C** in particular

1 The _____ in weather between my country and that in the
United Kingdom is very noticeable.

A contrast   **B** compare   **C** comparison

2 The United Kingdom and my country _____ a lot in many
respects.

A different   **B** differentiate   **C** differ

3 A lot of British people are not aware that there is a big
_____ between the Spanish and Portuguese languages.

A different   **B** difference   **C** differ

4 I find it difficult to _____ between British English and
American English.

A distinctive   **B** extinguish   **C** distinguish

5 There's a big _____ between learning a language and
actually using it.

A distinction   **B** distinctive   **C** distinguish

6 In my country, it is illegal to _____ between men and women.

A difference   **B** discipline   **C** discriminate

7 My country covers a large area. _____ , the United Kingdom
is quite small.

A By similar means   **B** By way of contrast   **C** In the same way

8 Customs in my country are _____ to those in the United Kingdom.

A common **B** similar **C** same

---

9 As far as I can tell, young people in the United Kingdom are physically _____ to young people in my country. They look exactly the same.

A identical **B** similar **C** same

---

10 In my country, people live to eat, _____ in the United Kingdom people eat to live.

A therefore **B** where **C** whereas

---

11 Young people in my country share the same interests as those in the United Kingdom, but in other respects we are as different as _____ .

A rain and sun **B** chalk and cheese **C** hot and cold

---

12 Physically, my country is quite close to the United Kingdom, but culturally we are _____ .

A worlds apart **B** years away
C two sandwiches short of a picnic.

In the exam ...

If you are doing the exam in the United Kingdom or another English-speaking country, you may be asked, especially in the Speaking Test, to talk about the differences between your country and the one you are in now. Language of contrast and comparison is also useful to talk about people, and you might find some of the expressions useful if you decide to write a discursive composition, article or report in the Writing Paper.

See also: Test 58 Writing a report

Test 59 Writing a composition or article

4 Confusing words

Complete the following sentences with the correct word. There is an example at the beginning (0).

0 My teacher gave me some very useful _____*advice*_____ .
advice/advise

1 Twenty years ago, very few people owned computers, but
_____ a lot of people have them. **actually/now**

2 My poor pronunciation sometimes _____ my ability
to communicate in English. **affects/effects**

3 I haven't seen her _____ this morning. **already/yet**

4 I have always been _____ snakes and spiders.
worried about/afraid of

5 My limited vocabulary _____ me from getting a good
grade in the FCE. **avoided/prevented**

6 At three o'clock, I _____ the children from school.
bring/fetch

7 If you learn the vocabulary in this book, you have a better
_____ of passing the FCE. **chance/possibility**

8 My English isn't so good. I'm always making _____
mistakes. **continuous/continual**

9 Last summer we had a _____ holiday in Italy.
formidable/wonderful

10 'Did you enjoy the party?' 'Yes, it was _____ .'
fun/funny

11 I _____ swimming and running every day. **go/play**

12 Molly asked me if I would like to _____ her to the cinema. **go with/follow**

13 You can borrow my car, but if you _____ it, I'll never talk to you again! **harm/damage**

14 I like working here. It's a good _____ . **job/work**

15 She's such a _____ girl; she's always helping people. **kind/sympathetic**

16 I asked him to _____ me £20 until Monday. **borrow/lend**

17 My mother asked me to _____ the table. **lay/lie**

18 I love being in the _____ in spring. **countryside/nature**

19 I thought the painting was worth a lot of money, but in fact it was _____ . **priceless/worthless**

20 I sat on the beach at dawn and watched the sun _____ . **raise/rise**

21 When we go to town, could you _____ me to buy some milk? **remember/remind**

22 From the top of the hill, you have a marvellous _____ of the town. **view/scenery**

23 He's a _____ boy and gets upset easily. **sensible/sensitive**

24 When you come to school tomorrow, don't forget to _____ your dictionary. **bring/take**

5 'Make', 'do' and 'take'

Complete these sentences using the verbs *make*, *do* or *take*. In many cases, you will need to change the form of the verb. In one case, more than one answer is possible. There is an example at the beginning (0).

0 They're _____ *making* _____ a lot of noise, but so far they haven't _____ *made* _____ any progress.

1 The company is _____ a large profit, but in the meantime they're _____ a lot of damage to the environment.

2 She was asked to _____ a quick speech, but she _____ her time.

3 After we've _____ our homework, we should _____ the washing up.

4 _____ a look at all these mistakes you've _____ !

5 Shall we _____ a taxi or go by train?

6 At first, he _____ a great effort to _____ an interest in his lessons.

7 This is a photograph I _____ of some friends we _____ when we were on holiday.

8 She told me to _____ a seat, and then went to _____ some phone calls.

9 _____ a test is a bit like _____ a crossword: you finish it eventually!

10 The policeman _____ my name and address, and
_____ a few notes.

11 We had to _____ a lot of work before we began to
_____ any money.

12 The conference _____ place in January, and since
then we've _____ a lot of business with the other
companies there.

13 You should really _____ my advice and hire
somebody to _____ your ironing, washing and other
housework.

14 After I had _____ the bed, he lay down and
_____ his medicine.

15 It won't _____ any harm to _____ some
enquiries.

16 Our company _____ a loss in its first year, but now
we're _____ well.

In the exam ...

Students often misuse words like *make, do* and *take*. It is often *small*
mistakes like these that stop them from getting a good grade in the FCE. A
lot of students concentrate on learning *individual* words and ignore the
other words that work *with* them. Another good example of this is the use
of prepositions.

See also: Test 16 Prepositions

6 Get 1

The word *get* is used a lot in English. Look at these following sentences and replace the words in bold with a suitable verb which you will find hidden in the word grid opposite. There is an example at the beginning (0).

| 0 | I haven't heard from you for ages; did you **get** my last letter? | *receive* |

| 1 | I want to **get** a good grade in my FCE. | _____ |

| 2 | As people **get** older, they tend to need less sleep. | _____ |

| 3 | He told me a joke, but I didn't **get** it. | _____ |

| 4 | I decided to **get** a new bicycle. | _____ |

| 5 | We're a bit late. I think we should **get going**. | _____ |

| 6 | She's so lazy. It really **gets** me. | _____ |

| 7 | We didn't **get to** London until after dark. | _____ |

| 8 | If you **get** dinner, I'll wash up afterwards. | _____ |

| 9 | I have a summer job, but I don't **get** much. | _____ |

| 10 | I managed to **get** my brother to help me with my homework. | _____ |

| 11 | I've left my dictionary in the classroom. Could you **get** it for me? | _____ |

| 12 | My computer has been broken for a few days. I must **get** it repaired. | _____ |

13 I didn't **get** to see my teacher before the exam. _____

14 I usually **get off** work at about five o'clock. _____

15 The party lasted for ages, and we didn't
get away until almost midnight. _____

16 I don't think we'll **get anywhere** with
this idea. _____

17 Cold, wet weather **gets** me **down**. _____

18 If you want to **get into** university, you'll
have to work hard. _____

19 We decided to **get together** after work. _____

A	R	B	D	E	P	R	E	S	S	E	S	S	D	F
M	E	E	T	N	G	H	J	U	K	A	L	M	N	B
A	C	C	Q	T	H	W	E	C	R	R	E	A	C	H
N	E	O	L	E	A	V	E	C	A	N	N	O	Y	S
A	I	M	C	R	V	V	B	E	O	N	B	T	U	F
G	V	E	H	J	E	L	P	E	R	S	U	A	D	E
E	E	S	T	A	R	T	Q	D	I	W	Y	E	R	T
V	C	X	Z	A	C	H	I	E	V	E	T	R	E	C
F	I	N	I	S	H	X	P	R	E	P	A	R	E	H
Y	T	U	N	D	E	R	S	T	A.	N	D	U	Y	F

7 Get 2

The following sentences all use **get**. Look at the definition which follows each one, and decide whether it is TRUE (T) or FALSE (F). There is an example at the beginning (0).

0 James and Tony <u>get along</u> with each other.

James and Tony don't like each other. T / (F)

1 Joanne is <u>getting over</u> her illness.

Joanne is recovering from her illness. T / F

2 Alice is <u>getting on</u> at university.

Alice is going to start university. T / F

3 The teacher gave us a test, and I managed to <u>get out of</u> it.

I received a good grade. T / F

4 Janet <u>got her own back</u> on Susan for breaking her camera.

Janet took revenge on Susan. T/ F

5 Mr. Walton must be <u>getting on for</u> sixty.

Mr. Walton is over sixty years old. T / F

6 I tried to <u>get through to</u> the sales department, but was cut off.

I tried to visit the sales department. T / F

7 I couldn't <u>get into</u> the book I was supposed to read for the FCE.

I couldn't find the book I was supposed to read for the FCE.

T / F

8 Sometimes, Jeanette <u>gets my back up</u>.

Sometimes, Jeanette annoys me. T / F

9   This homework is really difficult. Let's <u>get it over with</u>.

Let's not do this homework.   T / F

10   Mark is always <u>getting at</u> me.

Mark is always criticizing me.   T/ F

11   He stole lots of money, and <u>got away with it</u>.

He stole lots of money, and ran away.   T / F

12   Whatever I say to Bob, I can't seem to <u>get through to</u> him.

Bob can't hear me.   T / F

13   I think Sean <u>got out of bed on the wrong side</u> this morning.

I think Sean woke up late this morning.   T / F

14   When I tried to explain the situation to Rebecca, she <u>got hold of the wrong end of the stick</u>.

Rebecca misunderstood me.   T / F

15   The teacher told me to <u>get my act together</u>.

The teacher told me to get myself organized and start working.   T / F

16   'Come on! <u>Get a grip on yourself</u>!'

'Stop misbehaving!'   T / F

17   '<u>Get away</u>!'

'I don't believe you!'   T / F

18   '<u>Get a life</u>!'

'Start looking after yourself.'   T / F

8 Abstract nouns

Abstract nouns are nouns which we normally cannot *see*, *hear*, *touch*, *smell* or *taste*. Complete these sentences with an appropriate abstract noun formed from the word in **bold**. There is an example at the beginning (0).

0 She's in a position of great ___*responsibility*___ . **responsible**

1 When I walked in, she looked at me in _____ .

astonish

2 His _____ came as a great shock to all of us. **die**

3 There have been a lot of _____ in science and technology in the last twenty years. **develop**

4 His sudden _____ was a complete mystery.

disappear

5 I made a remarkable _____ when I opened the box. **discover**

6 We reported the _____ of our car to the police.

lose

7 Did you get _____ to leave early? **permit**

8 If your _____ doesn't improve, you'll have to leave the school. **behave**

9 When his trousers fell down, the whole room shook with _____ . **laugh**

10 Her face went bright red with _____ . **embarrass**

11 It's been a _____ meeting you. **please**

12 Don't forget to put your _____ at the bottom of the paper. **sign**

13 I would like to make a _____ about the service in your restaurant. **complain**

14 After dinner, she made an important _____ .

announce

15 I'm afraid my English _____ isn't very good.

pronounce

16 If you want to achieve _____ in the FCE, you will need to study hard.

succeed

17 British Airways announce the _____ of flight BA671 from Bangkok.

arrive

18 The _____ begins at exactly half past seven.

perform

19 I had a terrible _____ with my boyfriend. **argue**

20 As far as I'm concerned, _____ is more important than money.

happy

21 Do you think that there's too much _____ on television?

violent

22 If you can't stand the _____ , get out of the kitchen.

hot

23 I'm afraid I don't have much _____ with lazy people.

patient

24 Do French, Italian and Spanish have any _____ ?

similar

25 He didn't show much _____ when I told him I had split up with my girlfriend.

sympathetic

26 He always seems to have a lot of _____ .

confident

27 In all _____ he'll pass the FCE. **probable**

28 The mountain reaches a _____ of almost 6,000 metres.

high

9 Adjectives formed from nouns and verbs

Complete each sentence with an appropriate form of the word in **bold**.
There is an example at the beginning (0).

0	Make sure you have something _**constructive**_ to say before you stand up and speak.	**construct**
1	The work of cabin crew on an aircraft is often seen as an _____ job.	**attract**
2	A new _____ centre is being built outside the town.	**industry**
3	Trees are being cut down to provide _____ parking spaces.	**addition**
4	The school is located in a quiet _____ area.	**resident**
5	Waddesdon Manor is a _____ example of a nineteenth century stately home.	**beauty**
6	I don't think your demands are very _____ .	**reason**
7	She was a very _____ woman.	**ambition**
8	In the 1920s she became the _____ owner of a large country estate.	**wealth**
9	When I first came to England I was very _____ .	**loner**
10	An _____ thing happened to me yesterday.	**amuse**
11	Exercise can be _____ provided you do not overdo it.	**benefit**
12	We had an _____ time at the party.	**enjoy**
13	Swimming is an _____ way of keeping fit.	**effect**

14   For some people, losing weight can develop into a
_____ obsession.   **danger**

15   Our town library is facing serious _____ problems.
   finance

16   Some people remain _____ well into their eighties.
   act

17   British weather can be very _____ .   **change**

18   She was very _____ about her bad behaviour.
   apology

19   The police became _____ when he started to
tell lies.   **suspect**

20   Writing a book can be a very _____ experience.
   satisfy

21   We were so _____ during the lesson.   **bore**

22   Last year's show was a disaster, but this year's was a
_____ success.   **compare**

23   He had lost so much weight he was hardly _____ .
   recognise

24   My cousin is very _____ and loves playing sports.
   compete

25   _____ people are often sad and uncommunicative.
   create

26   Going on holiday is _____ to staying at home.   **prefer**

27   The management think they will succeed, but I am rather
_____ .   **doubt**

28   People living in small villages need a _____ public
transport system.   **depend**

29   It was a very _____ film.   **disappoint**

10 Directions

Follow these directions on the map opposite and see where you end up.
There is an example at the beginning (0).

0   You are at the station, which is shown by the letter A
on the map. Leave the station and turn left. Turn left
at the crossroads, go through the tunnel and take the
first road on your right. It's at the end of the road.   *E*

1   You are starting at the station. Can you see it on the
map? It's shown by the letter 'A'. Leave the station and
turn left. Take the first road on your right. It's on the
left. You can't miss it.   _____

2   From here, continue walking to the crossroads. At the
crossroads, go straight across and continue walking. It's on
your left, on the corner.   _____

3   Go back the way you came, and at the crossroads, turn
left. Continue straight ahead, past the traffic lights and
over the bridge. Go right at the fork and keep walking
until you find the cul-de-sac. It's at the end of the
cul-de-sac.   _____

4   Leave the cul-de-sac and turn left. Take the first road on
your left and, at the second crossroads, turn right. Keep
going until you find a roundabout. Turn left at the
roundabout and then immediately right. Follow the
road round to your left. It's at the end of this road.   _____

5   Go back the way you came until you get to the
roundabout. At the roundabout, turn left and keep
walking until you find the second road on your left.
Go down this road and take the second road on
your right. It's straight ahead, at the end of the road.   _____

6 Go back the way you came until you get to the T-junction. At the T-junction, turn right and then immediately left. Go through the tunnel and, at the second crossroads, turn right. Go straight ahead and take the first road on your left. At the end of this road, turn right. Keep going until you get to the next T-junction and turn left again. You'll find it at the end of the second road on your left. _____

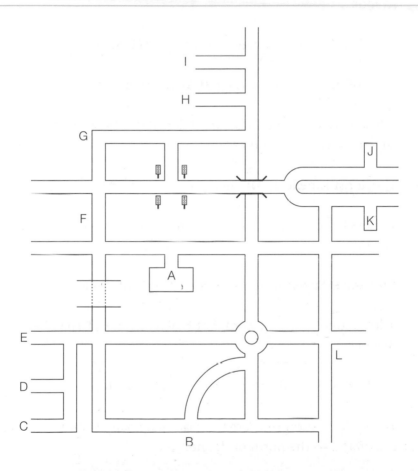

In the exam ...

You may need to give directions in a letter or a report. In addition to knowing how to give directions, you will also need to know the English words for the different things we find in the street, such as *traffic lights*, *junctions* and *roundabouts*.

See also: Test 11 Location

11 Location

Where's the English school? Work it out by reading these sentences and writing the names of the places on the map opposite. There is an example at the beginning (0).

0   Peach Street runs from the underground station to Thatcher Avenue.

1   Thatcher Avenue is at right angles to Peach Street.

2   The hospital is opposite the fast food restaurant.

3   'Mr. Greasy's' fast food restaurant is halfway between 'Supersave Supermarket' and 'Club Latino'.

4   The florist is next to 'Mr Greasy's'.

5   Visitors to Pogle Park have somewhere to buy ice cream and cold drinks.

6   'Supersave' Supermarket is on the left side of Peach Street.

7   'Club Latino' is on the corner of Peach Street and Thatcher Avenue.

8   The library is beside 'Harridge's' department store.

9   The police station is across the road diagonally from the fast food restaurant, to the north of the hospital.

10   Searle Street runs parallel to Peach Street.

11   Pogle Park is at the end of Searle Street.

12   The underground station is in the middle of Walton Square.

13 Walton Square is at the south end of Peach Street.

14 The sports shop is to the east of the police station.

15 Gruchy Lane connects Walton Square with Pogle Park.

16 'Harridge's' department store is on the right side of Peach Street near Walton Square.

17 'Nibbles' café is surrounded by a small wood.

18 'Club Latino' is *not* on the same side of the road as 'Harridge's'.

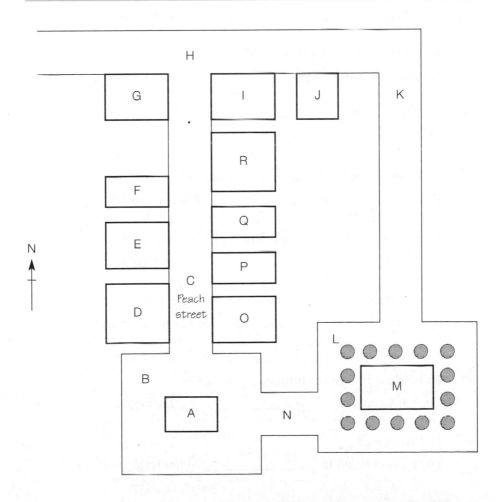

12 Changes

Look at the definitions and the sample sentences, and complete the table on page 24 with the appropriate word. The first and last letter of each word have been given to you. There is an example at the beginning (0).

0   To make something suitable for a new need or purpose.

The author is going to _____ adapt _____ his novel for television.

1   To correct or slightly change the position of something else.

You need to _____ your tie; it's not straight.

2   To change in some way.

I wanted to _____ the terms of my contract.

3   To bring health to some one who is ill.

I hoped the medicine would _____ me of my cold.

4   To lower someone in rank or position, often as a punishment.

My boss threatened to _____ if I didn't work harder.

5   To move so that you cannot see or find it.

When did the money _____ from your briefcase?

6   To make or become a liquid when put into a liquid.

First of all, _____ some sugar in hot water.

7   To give something to someone who then gives you something else.

If your new trousers are too tight, take them to the shop and _____ them.

8   To increase in size or number.

The school has decided to _____ the English Department.

9   To lose colour.

The pictures began to _____ in the bright sunlight.

10   To become larger in amount or number.

Over the next few years, we will see a large _____ in the number of unemployed.

11   The opposite of 4 above.

If you work hard, they might _____ you.

12   To make less in size or amount.

If you _____ the price, I'll buy it.

13   To begin something again.

Membership lasts for one year, after which you have to _____ it.

14   To repair something and put it back into good condition.

The old cinema will be much better when they _____ it.

15   To change one thing for another that is newer or better.

I decided to _____ my old dictionary.

16   To become larger and rounder.

After the wasp stung me, I watched my hand _____ up.

17   To change one thing for another thing.

If you're not happy with what you do at work, why don't you ask your manager if you can _____ jobs.

18   To change something completely in form, appearance or nature.

It would be nice if we could _____ the car park into a public garden.

19   To be, make or become different.

You shouldn't just eat hamburgers; you should try to _____ your diet.

#									
0	A	D	A	P	T				
1	A					T			
2	A				R				
3	C			E					
4	D					E			
5	D							R	
6	D						E		
7	E						E		
8	E					D			
9	F			E					
10	I						E		
11	P						E		
12	R					E			
13	R			W					
14	R						E		
15	R					E			
16	S			L					
17	S				H				
18	T								M
19	V		Y						

Several of these words can have more than one meaning. Use your dictionary to find which ones.

In the exam ...

Try not to use the same word too often. In the test above, all of the words in the table are different meanings of the word *change*. You should try to develop a list and remember synonyms for other words. Good examples of these include *walk*, *look*, *nice* and *speak*, all of which have a lot of synonyms. *The Longman Language Activator* is a good source of alternative words which will help your English to become more fluent.

See also: Test 2 Actions

13 Opposites 1

Change these words using the prefixes in the box so that they have an opposite meaning. There is an example at the beginning (0).

mis-	un-	dis-	ir-	il-	in-	im-

0	_in_ correct	16	____qualified	32	____personal
1	____believable	17	____avoidable	33	____complete
2	____obedient	18	____competent	34	____accurate
3	____adequate	19	____conscious	35	____legal
4	____honest	20	____certain	36	____agreeable
5	____acceptable	21	____attractive	37	____possible
6	____perfect	22	____patient	38	____mature
7	____regular	23	____fair	39	____satisfied
8	____ responsible	24	____married	40	____logical
9	____limited	25	____fashionable	41	____comfortable
10	____even	26	____welcome	42	____agree
11	____like (verb)	27	____behave	43	____obey
12	____understand	28	____trust (verb)	44	____approve
13	____pronounce	29	____wrap	45	____pack
14	____lock	30	____continue	46	____cover
15	____connect	31	____fold	47	____appear

14 Opposites 2

Complete these sentences with an opposite of the verb in **bold**. In some cases, more than one answer is possible. Make sure that you use the correct form of each verb. There is an example at the beginning (0).

| 0 | Although we **missed** our train to the airport, we still _____*caught*_____ the plane. |

| 1 | We didn't **spend** much money. In fact, we managed to _____ a lot. |

| 2 | The train **arrives** at the station at 4 o'clock and _____ five minutes later. |

| 3 | After he had **emptied** the bottle, he _____ it with water. |

| 4 | 'Can you **lend** me £10?' 'No way. The last time you _____ money from me, you didn't pay it back!' |

| 5 | She isn't **laughing**, she's _____ . |

| 6 | The principal doesn't **allow** smoking at school. In fact, he _____ anything that is bad for our health. |

| 7 | 'Did he **confess** to stealing your money?' 'No, he _____ everything.' |

| 8 | In summer, the sun **rises** at about five o'clock and doesn't _____ until after nine in the evening. |

| 9 | He didn't **pass** the exam. In fact, he _____ with a very low score. |

10   At first, his business **succeeded**, but after the recession it
_____ dramatically.

11   She threw the ball to me, but **missed** and _____ the
window instead.

12   Our teacher **rewarded** all the good students, but decided to
_____ the bad ones.

13   'Did you **remember** to buy some milk?' 'Oh, sorry, I
_____ .'

14   Although I **sent** the letter on Monday, she didn't
_____ it until Friday.

15   My local council **demolished** the old flats and _____
some new ones.

16   We thought we would **lose** the game, but to our surprise we
_____ .

17   I hoped she would **agree** to meet me, but she _____ .

18   If you are **attacked** in the street, there are several different ways
you can _____ yourself.

19   She spends too much time **playing** and not enough time
_____ .

15 Opposites 3

Complete these sentences with an opposite of the adjective in **bold**. There is an example at the beginning (0).

0 A cricket ball is **solid**, but a table-tennis ball is ___*hollow*___ .

1 Her pearls are **real**, but her eyelashes are _____ .

2 This bread isn't **fresh**, it's _____ .

3 Do you prefer listening to **live** music or _____ music?

4 The chair is very **hard**. Put a _____ cushion on it.

5 This knife isn't **sharp**, it's completely _____ .

6 She was wearing a **dark** blue skirt and a _____ yellow blouse.

7 Those trousers are too **tight** for me but these are too _____ . Have you got another pair?

8 My steak was very **tender**, but hers was a bit _____ .

9 There are some things you can do in **private** that you should never do in _____ .

10 At the end of the long, **dim** tunnel, we could see a _____ light shining.

11 The **deep** lake was surrounded by a series of _____ pools.

12 It was only a **temporary** job until I could find something more _____ .

13 I had a **heavy** lunch, so I only want a _____ meal for dinner.

14 The thief said he was **innocent**, but the judge decided he was _____ .

15 The students were all **early**, but the teacher was _____ .

16 Half the students were **present**, the other half were _____ .

17 My sister is very **hardworking**, but my brother is very _____ .

18 Attendance at class is **compulsory**, but the afternoon social programme is _____ .

19 I don't like it when the sea is **rough**; I prefer it when it's _____ .

20 The room is about ten metres **long** and four metres _____ .

21 My best friend is quite **mean**, but his sister is very _____ .

22 There has been a **major** accident, but fortunately there have only been a few _____ injuries.

23 I prefer **strong** coffee to _____ coffee.

16 Prepositions

Complete these groups of sentences with a preposition (*in*, *on*, *at*, etc.). The same preposition can be used for each sentence in the group. There is an example at the beginning (0).

0   I don't enjoy travelling ____*by*____ car or boat.

I took the wrong coat ____*by*____ mistake.

The lesson had started ____*by*____ the time I arrived.

1   There's a ladder leaning _____ the wall.

I have always been _____ hunting.

I decided to become a dancer _____ my parents' wishes.

2   I'm ashamed _____ my poor English.

They accused us _____ stealing their money.

I've never approved _____ smoking.

3   We decided to share the chocolate _____ ourselves.

I love being _____ a large group of people.

Unemployment is high _____ young men under 25.

4   Let's buy him something nice _____ his birthday _____ a change.

You ought to apologize _____ your bad behaviour.

Are you responsible _____ breaking my stereo?

5   _____ the end of the test, don't forget to put your name _____ the top of the page.

I've always been quite good _____ swimming.

My town is always very quiet _____ night, especially _____ Christmas.

6 What time does the train arrive _____ London?

My brother always confides _____ me when he has a secret.

I'm interested _____ history, and have always succeeded _____ getting good results.

7 There was a lot of noise _____ the concert.

_____ the summer holiday, I like to relax and take things easy.

I heard strange noises _____ the night.

8 I look forward _____ hearing from you soon.

I have always objected _____ people who interrupt me.

Occasionally I need some time _____ myself.

9 My sister always relies _____ me to help her.

I'm not very keen _____ maths.

I think he started the fire _____ purpose.

10 British people get annoyed _____ you if you don't stand in line at the bus stop.

Some people are unable to cope _____ pressure.

The police charged him _____ murder.

11 The computer suddenly burst _____ flames.

How many times does 4 go _____ 44.

When I walked _____ the room, everyone went silent.

12 Some people like to complain _____ everything.

She's _____ twenty-five or twenty-six years old.

There's something very strange _____ our teacher.

17 Shapes and features

Look at the following descriptions, and choose an object from the pictures opposite that best suits each description, using the words in bold to help you. There is an example at the beginning (0).

0   A **pyramid** with **steep** sides.   _____f_____

1   A **crescent** with a **rough** surface.   _____

2   A **flat rectangle** with words and numbers on one side.   _____

3   A **long**, **thin rectangle** made of metal, with a **jagged** edge and a **sharp** end.   _____

4   A small edible **cone** with a **rough** surface.   _____

5   A **solid** plastic or wooden **cube** with **dots** on each side.   _____

6   A **square** with a **flat, chequered** surface.   _____

7   An edible **oval**, with a **smooth** surface.   _____

8   A **spiral** made of metal with **pointed** ends.   _____

9   A plastic **circle** with a **rough** top.   _____

10 A large **sphere** made of gas.   _____

11 A **hard hollow cylinder** with open ends.   _____

12 A **triangle** at both ends, with **soft** nylon sides.   _____

13 An **irregular-shaped hollow** object with **knobbly** sides.   _____

The Sun

18 Time

Complete the sentences with the most appropriate word or expression from the box. In some cases, more than one answer is possible. There is an example at the beginning (0).

throughout	ever since	back in	following	earlier	during
~~one day~~	in the meantime	formerly	by the time	over	while
from now on	once	as soon as	previously	when	meanwhile

0 ___*One day*___ I hope to be rich and successful.

1 _____ I arrived at school, the lesson had begun.

2 _____ he had explained it to me, I understood how it worked.

3 The Russian Federation was _____ known as the Soviet Union.

4 He was lying in hospital with a broken leg. Two hours _____ , he had been skiing.

5 _____ I was having a shower, the phone rang.

6 I was having a shower _____ the phone suddenly rang.

7 _____ the lesson, I listened to my Walkman.

8 When I'm rich, I'll buy a Ferrari. _____ , I'll continue to drive my old Fiat.

9 _____ the earthquake, thousands of people were homeless.

10 _____ the singer walked onto the stage, everyone started clapping and cheering.

11 _____ the past few weeks, I've learned a lot of vocabulary.

12 _____ the 1980s, very few people owned computers.

13 I've loved her _____ I first saw her.

14 I know I haven't been working so hard recently, but _____ I promise to try harder, starting right here.

19 Clothes and fashion 1

Read the following sentences about getting ready for an important interview and choose the most appropriate word or expression from those in **bold**. There is an example at the beginning (0).

0 It takes me such a long time every morning to get up and **put on / get dressed / wear**. I've got an important job interview this morning, however, so I need to hurry up.

1 Perhaps I should **get dressed / try on / put on** my purple tie.

2 And maybe I'll **try on / get dressed / wear** my new green trousers.

3 Oh no! They don't **suit / fit / measure** me. They're too short!

4 It's my own fault. I didn't **try them on / wear them out / fit them up** before I bought them.

5 And I really should have **creased / crumpled / ironed** them.

6 Now, which jacket shall I wear? Perhaps the blue one – it really **matches / suits / equals** me.

7 As for shoes, I can't wear those black shoes – they don't **match / fit / measure** my orange shirt. I'll wear my red trainers instead.

8 This waistcoat is too small for me now. I've **grown out of / grown into / grown over** it. I know – I'll wear my pink cardigan instead.

9 Unfortunately I haven't got any socks: I wore them all **out / off / on**.

10 Oh no, I can't **do in / do over / do up** the zip on my trousers. Oh well, nobody will notice.

11 OK, finished. Now let's take a look at myself in the mirror. Oh dear, I'm certainly no **grandmodel / supermodel / greatmodel**.

12 Oh well, it's too late to **alter / change / exchange** now.

20 Clothes and fashion 2

Read the descriptions of the different outfits worn by each person, and choose the appropriate picture, A, B or C, for each description.

1 Susan is wearing high-heeled shoes, tights, a knee-length skirt, a blouse with a floral pattern, a necklace and earrings.

2 Mary is wearing sandals, baggy trousers, a V-necked jumper, a spotted silk scarf and a silver bracelet.

A   B   C   A   B   C

3 Jemima is wearing boots, a pair of jeans, a woollen jacket, gloves and a hat.

4 Robert is dressed in a double-breasted jacket with striped trousers, a waistcoat and a spotted tie.

A   B   C   A   B   C

5   Jim is wearing trainers, tight jeans, a striped sweatshirt and a baseball cap.

A   B   C

6   George is wearing checked baggy shorts held up with a belt, a pair of sandals with long spotted socks, a plain T-shirt and a beret.

A   B   C

7   Maureen is wearing slippers, a pleated skirt, a long, striped overcoat and a pair of mittens.

A   B   C

8   Eddie is casually dressed in a pair of comfortable shoes, chinos and a tartan polo-necked jumper.

A   B   C

See also: Test 21 Describing personality
Test 47 Physical appearance

21 Describing personality

Read the following descriptions of eight different people, and write their names in the appropriate box depending on their personality. The first one has been done as an example.

A Name: _Betty_	B Name: _____	C Name: _____	D Name: _____
tetchy bossy conceited bigoted bitchy	reliable punctual industrious timid absent-minded	stoical witty impulsive garrulous gregarious	mean obstinate generous changeable obedient

E Name: _____	F Name: _____	G Name: _____	H Name: _____
optimistic independent cheerful artistic easy-going	intellectual suspicious pessimistic untidy lazy	romantic sensitive energetic creative adventurous	popular honest ambitious open-minded friendly

1 My girlfriend Julie is always doing something. When she isn't making things with her hands, she is risking her life doing dangerous activities like parachuting or bungee jumping. She loves it when I buy her flowers, take her out or say nice things about her, but she gets very upset if I say anything horrible to her.

2 My sister Molly seems to be a different person every day! Sometimes she will be buying presents for everyone, and at other times she resents spending even the smallest amount of money. One day she will do whatever people tell her to do, the next day she refuses to even listen to them, especially once she's made her mind up about something.

3   Betty has a very high opinion of herself and is always saying nasty things about other people. She gets irritated very quickly and likes to tell people what to do. She also believes, often unreasonably, that she is right and best, especially in matters of religion, politics or race.

4   Charlie has always wanted to be a painter. He loves to do his own thing, and rarely loses his temper. He always seems to be happy, and has great hopes for the future.

5   Richard says he wants to be Prime Minister one day, but I doubt he would be a good politician. Why? Well, for a start he always tells the truth. Secondly, he gets on well with everybody, and everyone likes him. And above all, he is very tolerant of other people.

6   Mary is always expecting bad things to happen, and never trusts strangers. She never seems to do any work and her room is always a mess. She likes to spend her time reading academic textbooks.

7   Joanne is very sociable and enjoys the company of other people. She tends to talk a lot, but she often makes clever or amusing remarks. She often does things without thinking of the consequences, but always manages to remain calm when things go wrong.

8   Bob is easily frightened, especially of his boss, which is probably why he's never late for work. He is often so concerned with his own thoughts that he forgets things. On the other hand, he works hard and is somebody you can trust and depend on at all times.

22 Friends and relations 1

A Read the text below, and write the names in the family tree using the key words in **bold** to help you. One of them has been done as an example.

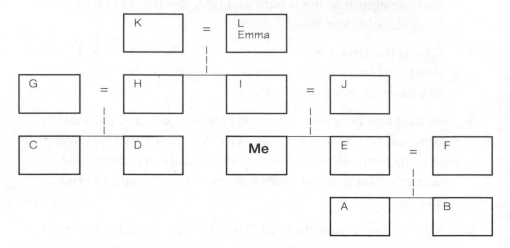

I come from a fairly close-knit family, although we don't always get on too well. I am very *close* to my **grandmother**, Emma, especially as we *have a lot in common*, but I've recently *fallen out with* my **grandfather**, John. Their **son** is my **father**, Bob. He's quite old-fashioned, and we don't always *see eye to eye*; I know I should *look up to him* as a role model, but the fact is I *don't respect* him very much. On the other hand, I *worship* my **mother**, Maureen; she's kind, caring and very tolerant of others. I have one younger **sister**, Sally, who I'm quite *fond of*, and I *admire* my **brother-in-law**, Andrew, who is a very talented painter. I have a precocious **nephew**, Tony, who I'm a *bit fed up with*, and a lovely little **niece**, Claudia, whom I *adore*. My father has a sister – my **aunt** Sue. I *respect* her, as she's had to put up with a lot of hardship in life, especially being married to my **uncle** Stanley, who treats her terribly. I must confess I *loathe* him. I also *despise* his son, my **cousin** Stuart, who takes after his father. My older **cousin** Claire, on the other hand, I *idolise*.

B   Read the text again and write the names of the different people in the appropriate box below, depending on how the writer feels about them. Use the words and expressions in italics to help you. One has been done as an example.

The writer feels positive about these people	The writer feels negative about these people
Emma (his grandmother)	

23 Friends and relations 2

Complete the sentences on the left with an appropriate word or expression on the right. There is an example at the beginning (0).

0	Laurence and I get on really well and do absolutely everything together. He is ...	... my ex-girlfriend.
1	I know Bob, but not very well. He is ...	... my fiancée.
2	Jenny and I work together in the same office. She is ...	... my workmate.
3	Jane and I announced our engagement last week and plan to get married in the summer. She is ...	... my flatmate.
4	Clare and I used to go out together. She is ...	... just good friends.
5	Susie and I have been going out together now for a few months. She is ...	... my best friend.
6	Jordi attends the same English lessons as me. He is ...	... my steady girlfriend.
7	Sarah works alongside me on the production line in a factory. She is ...	... a good friend.
8	John and I share an apartment in the city. He is ...	... my classmate.
9	I often go out with Ben to the cinema or the pub. He is ...	... an aquaintance.
10	Andy and I are are going out together, but we haven't told anybody yet. In fact, if anyone asks, we say that we are ...	... my colleague.

In the exam ...

You may be asked to talk about your family and friends in the Speaking Test or write about them in the Writing Paper. In addition to saying who they are, you can give information about their ages and occupations, their personality, what they look like, what kind of relationship you have with them, etc. You may also be asked to give an example of why, for example, you get on well with your best friend, or describe something that you did with your friends or family (for example, a story about a day out you had).

See also: Test 21 Describing personality

Test 47 Physical appearance

24 Travel and holidays 1

Complete the text with appropriate words or expressions from the box. There is an example at the beginning (0).

sightseeing	boarding card	lands	cabin crew	takes off
check out	book (verb)	departure lounge	board	gate
currency	tickets	check in	safety belt	suitcase
cheques	sunbathing	passport	duty free	customs
	~~travel agent's~~	brochures		

Going on holiday is great fun, and it's so easy! First of all go to the **0** _travel agent's_ and collect some **1** _____ . Pick the holiday you want and go back to the travel agent's to **2** _____ it. You'll receive your **3** _____ a week or so before you depart. Make sure that you have a valid **4** _____, some foreign **5** _____, some traveller's **6** _____ and some insurance. Pack your **7** _____ and then you're ready to go!

Go to the airport and **8** _____. The person at the desk will take your luggage and give you a **9** _____. This shows you your seat allocation. You then go through a security check and wait in the **10** _____ . If you like, you can browse around the **11** _____ shop. When your flight is called, go to the appropriate **12** _____ for your flight and **13** _____ your plane. The **14** _____ will help you find your seat. Don't forget to fasten your **15** _____ before the plane **16** _____.

When you get to your destination and the plane **17** _____, you disembark and pass through **18** _____, where you will have to show your passport. Collect your luggage and leave the airport. If you're on a package tour, there will probably be a coach to take you to your hotel. From then on, you can take things easy, **19** _____ on the beach and **20** _____ .

At the end of your holiday, you will need to **21** _____ of the hotel – make sure you return your key and settle any outstanding bills.

25 Travel and holidays 2

Complete these sentences with the appropriate word or expression from A, B, C or D. There is an example at the beginning (0).

0 If I had enough money, I would like to go on a round-the-world _____ .

(A) trip B travel C excursion D sightseeing

1 Make sure the train has stopped completely before you _____ .

A get down **B** get off C get away D get into

2 I enjoyed my holiday, but couldn't _____ the heat.

A put up with **B** put down C put up D put away

3 We couldn't _____ our minds where to go for our holiday, so we stayed at home!

A make out **B** make do C make up D make over

4 When I go on holiday, I like to _____ .

A take it simple **B** take it easy C take it relaxing D take it relaxed

5 Last year, we went on a two-week _____ around the Mediterranean.

A cruising **B** cruiser C cruise D crew

6 The accommodation on my last holiday was a bit _____ .

A basic **B** base C basically D bass

7 Don't forget to make a _____ for a room at least two weeks in advance.

A reserve **B** reserved C reserving D reservation

8 The _____ from London to Athens takes about three hours.

A flying **B** fly C flight D flies

9 We can't stay at the hotel because there aren't any _____ .

A vacant **B** vacancy C vacate D vacancies

10 I _____ some brochures from the travel agent's.

A picked off **B** picked up C picked on D picked out

11 It takes twenty hours for the ship to get from England to Spain, so it might be a good idea to book a _____ on board.

A resort **B** cabin C chalet D hostel

26 Travel and holidays 3

Match the different types of holiday in the box with the appropriate description 1–9 below. There is an example at the beginning (0).

> all-inclusive holiday   skiing holiday   safari   cruise
> ~~adventure holiday~~   package holiday   sightseeing holiday
> camping holiday   sailing holiday   hiking holiday

0   We had a great time. I went white-water rafting, bungee-jumping, gliding, and I even learnt how to parachute!

adventure holiday

1   This is a very popular kind of holiday. Basically, you pay for your flight, hotel accommodation and airport transfers before you leave, and then all you need to worry about when you get to your chosen destination are day-to-day expenses.

_____

2   We found a sheltered spot in the corner of the site and started to set up our tent. Unfortunately, we discovered that we had left the pegs at home! _____

3   Our cabin was very cramped, but we didn't mind too much as we spent most of our time on the deck and taking advantage of the ship's restaurants, bars and other facilities.

_____

4   We had a beautiful chalet at the foot of the slopes, and it was only a fifteen-minute cable-car journey to the top of the piste.

_____

5   At dusk we came to a watering hole where the animals had gathered to drink. The guide told us to stay in the jeep for our own safety, and also to prevent us frightening off the animals.

_____

6 The youth hostel was basic but clean, as everybody had to take off their boots before going inside. Of course, after a long day marching over muddy fields, these were absolutely filthy.

_____

7 We put on some warm clothes and a lifejacket and got onto the yacht. Unfortunately, we didn't get any further than the harbour as there was no wind!

_____

8 We spent a week in London and tried to see as much of it as possible; Buckingham Palace, the Tower of London, Trafalgar Square, you name it, we saw it. I must have taken hundreds of pictures.

_____

9 We paid £850 for the holiday. That price included flights, transfers, accommodation at a resort, entertainment and all our food and drinks.

_____

In the exam ...

In the Writing Paper you may be asked to describe a holiday you have had, a holiday you are planning or the type of holiday you would like to go on. You should try to include such information as the country, the kind of accommodation, the things you did/would do and if relevant, who you went with.

You may also have to write a letter, for example to a tour operator to ask for information about a holiday, to a friend giving them information about a holiday you would recommend, or to a hotel or tour operator to complain about a bad holiday you had.

27 Accommodation 1

Match the words below with their description. Then look at the adjectives in bold and put them into the appropriate section of the table depending on whether these words have a positive connotation (☺) or a negative connotation (☹). There is an example at the beginning (0).

caravan   country cottage   detached house   villa   bungalow
terraced house   castle   ~~tent~~   flat   mansion

0 Old ones were made of canvas and were very basic. Ours is made of nylon and can sleep three people. It's surprisingly **cosy**, and very easy to set up. However, it can get a bit **damp** if it rains.

tent

1 It's very impressive, isn't it? All those towers, turrets and ramparts. I would imagine that the rooms are very **spacious**, but I don't think anybody lives there anymore. There are probably no facilities, like electricity or running water. And it's probably very **draughty**.

2 It looks quite small, with probably just two or three rooms on each floor. They're probably a bit **cramped**, too. I'm not sure I'd like to live so close to my neighbours – you could hear everything that was going on on either side.

3 This is my idea of a typical modern family home. A living room, dining room and kitchen on the ground floor, three or four bedrooms and a bathroom upstairs, a garage and a small garden. It's not very **pretentious**, which is why I like it.

4 Who lives in a house like this? Probably somebody very rich. It's huge, isn't it? With those large windows, it's probably very **bright** and **airy** inside. And there's a long, tree-lined drive so that you can park your Rolls Royce collection.

5   I think it looks a bit **depressing**. I don't like high-rise accommodation. I imagine that the rooms are a bit **seedy** and **squalid**. It's not at all **homely**. I feel sorry for the people living there. _____

6   It's very pretty, with the garden and the flowers. It's probably a bit **basic** inside, and it might get a bit **claustrophobic** in the winter. A farmer might live here. Or maybe someone who has retired.

_____

7   Look at that patio and the fountain! And there's a balcony too. It's probably somebody's holiday home. I imagine that inside it's very **roomy** with lots of mod cons – air-conditioning, home entertainment system and so on. And lots of cool white marble on the floor. _____

8   It's quite small, but probably very **practical** for an elderly person who has problems getting up the stairs. It looks like there might be a small room in the attic, or it might just be storage space.

_____

9   It must be very **pokey** inside. It's OK for a holiday, but I'm surprised anybody could actually live here. I suppose the advantage is that if you get bored living in one place, you could just move, together with your home, somewhere else.

_____

☺ These words have a positive connotation	☹ These words have a negative connotation
cosy	

28 Accommodation 2

A Cover up the plan of the house at the bottom of this page, then read the description below. When you have done that, cover up the description and try to write the name of each feature into the plan.

I live in a bungalow on the outskirts of the city. There's a small, tree-lined **path** leading to the **porch**. As you go through the **front door**, you enter the **hall**. The first door on the right leads to the **kitchen-diner** and beyond that there's a small **utility room** where I keep the washing machine and fridge-freezer. The first door on the left leads to my **study**, where you'll find my desk and computer. Next to this room, there are some **stairs** leading down to the **cellar**, which I use for storage. After the stairs, also on the left, there's another door which goes through to the **living room**. Directly opposite this room is my **bedroom** and next to this there's a **bathroom**. The next room along is a small **bedsit**, with a bed and basic cooking facilities, which is being used by a student. At the end of the hall there's another door which opens out onto a small **terrace** and the **garden**, which has a few flowerbeds and a tiny lawn. There's a **shed** at the end of the garden where I keep my bicycle and gardening tools.

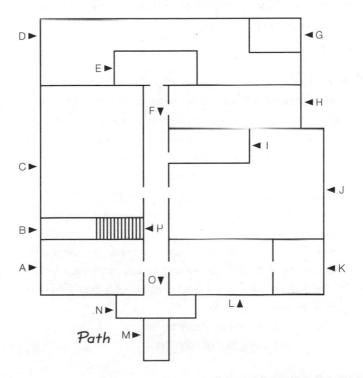

B Rearrange the mixed-up letters in **bold** in the following sentences to form an appropriate word.

0 If you can't afford to buy a flat, you will have to **tren** one.

_____ _rent_

1 Our landlord told us that if we didn't pay him immediately, he would **ticve** us.

_____

2 The local council are going to **medoshli** our apartment block as they claim it's dangerous.

_____

3 We wanted to buy a house, so applied to the bank for a **tromggae**.

_____

4 I think we should **rocedeta** the living room. What colour shall we paint it?

_____

5 As we have some spare offices, perhaps we could **seale** them to another company.

_____

In the exam …

In the Speaking Test you may be asked to describe your home or your 'dream' home, or you may be asked to describe a photograph of a house or other building. In addition to giving a brief description of the building, you should try to say what you think of it, who might live there and so on.

In the Writing Paper you might also be asked to describe a house in a letter or a report. In addition to describing the different rooms using a variety of adjectives, you may also need to explain where the rooms are in relation to each other.

Notice how the description of the house in part A is organised 'spatially' (it begins at the front of the house and moves to the back of the house). Try to do this if you are asked to talk or write about a room or a building.

See also: Test 11 Location

Test 17 Shapes and features

Test 54 Picture description

29 Animals and plants

SECTION 2

A   Look at this list of animals and plants, and put them into the table below, depending on their category. Some of them may belong in more than one category. There is an example for each category.

> ~~orchid~~   ~~oak~~   ~~cockroach~~   ~~tortoise~~   ~~horse~~   ~~penguin~~   ~~snake~~
> ~~octopus~~   ~~orang-utan~~   spider   daisy   chestnut   palm
> duck   tulip   cow   rabbit   eagle   bee   sheep   butterfly
> goat   cactus   crocodile   hamster   rose   rhinoceros
> whale   shark   trout   puppy   lizard   pigeon   ant   kitten
> white mouse   pig   bamboo   lobster   parrot   dolphin
> daffodil   tiger   panda   alligator

Pets/domestic animals	*tortoise*
Farm animals	*horse*
Birds	*penguin*
Endangered species	*orang-utan*
Reptiles	*snake*
Insects and invertebrates	*cockroach*
Fish and other water creatures	*octopus*
Flowers	*orchid*
Trees and other plants	*oak*

How many other words can you add to these categories?

Section 2: Topic vocabulary   **51**

B   Look at these descriptions of various animals and plants, and decide
what is being talked about (all the answers are on the previous page).
Use a dictionary to check the meanings of the words in bold, as these
will help you to decide what is being described. There is an example at
the beginning (0).

0   Children love them because they are quite **cuddly** and have big
floppy ears. I love them because they're delicious baked in a pie.

_____*rabbit*_____

1   They live in the southern hemisphere. They can't **fly**, but they
can **swim** very quickly and catch fish with their **beaks**. They live
in **colonies** of several thousand.   ___penguin___

2   This is a member of the **big-cat** family and comes from Asia. They
have very sharp **claws** and **fangs**, which they use to kill and eat
other animals.   ___tiger___

3   This is a **mammal**, although some people think it's a variety of
fish. Some of them can grow up to 30 metres in length.

___palm___

4   You find these on tropical beaches. They look beautiful, gently
swaying in the wind and providing sunbathers with welcome
shade. Watch out for falling **coconuts**!   ___puppy___

5   He's very **cute**, but he tends to make everything in the house
dirty with his muddy **paws**! Also, he never seems to stop **barking**.
He's very demanding, and I have to take him for a walk at least
twice a day.   ___rose___

6   My boyfriend bought me twelve red ones on my birthday. They're
beautiful, and have a pleasant **bouquet**. Watch out for the **thorns**
on the **stem** – they're very sharp. And don't touch the **petals** –
they break off really easily.   ___Kitten___

7   She was sitting in front of the fire, cleaning her **whiskers** and
purring loudly, but when she saw the dog, she starting **hissing**
and **spitting**.   ___oak___

8   They have large, spreading **branches**, deep **roots** and small,
irregular-shaped **leaves**. They can live to a very great age.

___snake___

9 People think they're **slimy**, but actually they're very dry to the touch. Some of them can be really **poisonous**, but they'll only **bite** you if you frighten them. _Tortoise_

10 They have a hard **shell**, which they hide in when they're frightened. They can't walk very quickly. Apparently, they can live to a very great age. _____

11 You must look after these animals a lot: make sure you clean their **hooves** regularly, and if you go riding, check that their shoes are in good condition. They love having their **mane** brushed. _____

12 They're delicious to eat, but you need to remove the **scales** and **gills** before you cook them. _____

13 With their large, colourful **wings**, these insects are beautiful. In the summer, my garden is full of them, **fluttering** around the flowers. _____

14 They're really useful animals. Not only can we eat their meat, we can also use their **wool** to make clothes. There are hundreds in a field near my house, and you can hear them **bleating** all the time. _____

15 With a loud **quacking** noise, they landed in the water and started **diving** for fish. _____

16 Thanks for offering to look after it for me while I'm away. Don't give it too much water – remember that it prefers dry **soil** – and whatever you do, don't touch the **spikes**; they're very sharp! _____

17 They're very **rare**. People try to **breed** them **in captivity**, but without much success. They may become **extinct** soon. _____

In the exam ...

Questions on wildlife and the environment are very popular. You might be asked to describe your favourite animal, or talk about animals and the role they play in our lives. You might also be asked to write a story involving animals, or an article on preserving wildlife.

See also: Test 38 The environment

30 Geography and the natural world

Test your knowledge of geography with this quiz.

0 Which of these **countries** has the highest **population**?

A India (B) China C Japan D the USA

1 Africa, South America and Asia are all examples of

_____ .

2 Hokkaido, Iceland and Ireland are examples of _____ .

3 Which of the following is <u>not</u> a mountain?

A Everest B Fuji C Mont Blanc D Manhattan

4 Choose the right word: The Himalayas, the Alps and the Andes are all examples of mountain **rangers / ranges / ranchers**.

5 Which of these rivers is the longest?

A The Thames B The Nile C The Amazon D The Mississippi

6 The Gobi, the Sahara and the Kalahari are all examples of

_____ .

7 The Atlantic, the Pacific, the Indian and the Arctic are all examples of _____ .

8 Choose the right word: Niagara, Angel and Victoria are all examples of **cascades / fountains / waterfalls**.

9 Choose the right word: The Suez and the Panama are examples of **canals / channels / chanels**.

10 Complete this sentence with an appropriate word: On our last holiday, we took a boat trip across _____ Geneva.

11 Complete this sentence with an appropriate word: Trees in the Amazon _____ are being cut down at an alarming rate.

12 What do you call the area of land between two groups of hills or mountains?

13 *Quito* is the only capital city which lies directly on the _____ .

14 Complete this sentence with an appropriate word: When the _____ erupted, the town had to be evacuated.

15 Complete this sentence with an appropriate word: The _____ blew for five days, destroying houses and blowing down trees. (More than one answer is possible.)

16 Complete this sentence with an appropriate word: The ground shook violently during the _____ .

17 What do we call a long period of hot, dry weather when crops and animals die?

 A a blizzard **B** a flood **C** a drought **D** a tidal wave
 E a tornado

18 Do polar bears live at the *North Pole* or the *South Pole*?

19 If a *hill* is a low mountain, what is a *stream*?

20 Which of these cities is <u>not</u> in the Northern hemisphere?

 A Bogota **B** Bombay **C** Jakarta **D** Panama **E** Colombo

See also: Test 31 Town and country
 Test 32 The weather
 Test 38 The environment

31 Town and country

Read the definitions and fill in the table opposite. There is an example at the beginning (0).

0	An adjective referring to towns and cities.
1	An adjective referring to the country.
2	A public place where people go for pleasure or entertainment.
3	A person who regularly travels to a town or city for work.
4	Periods during the day when people are travelling to and from work in a city (2 words).
5	A stretch of land around a city where building is not allowed (2 words).
6	An outer area of a city where people live.
7	Dirty air caused by traffic fumes, industry, noise, etc.
8	Evening entertainment such as bars and clubs in towns and cities.
9	The blocking of streets with traffic.
10	Plants, animals, earth, the weather, etc.
11	An adjective describing the pressures caused by the difficulties of life, which make you feel worried or tense.
12	Full of people.
13	Quiet and untroubled.
14	Not dangerous.
15	Consisting of people from many different parts of the world.
16	An area of land on a farm used for animals or crops.
17	The practice of farming.
18	A piece of land on which many different buildings of the same type have been built.
19	A very tall, modern city building.
20	A large building divided into separate parts, e.g., an office _____ or a _____ of flats.
21	Manufacturing companies or other types of commercial activity.

#									
0	U	R	B	A	N				
1		R		L					
2	A		E			Y			
3	C		M						
4		U				U			
5			E		B				
6				R	B				
7		O	L						
8				H		I	E		
9				E				N	
10	N				E				
11		T		E					
12			O		D				
13		E				U			
14		A							
\15			S	M			L		N
16				L	D				
17	A				U	L		R	
18			T		E				
19		K			C		A		
20			O	C					
21	I				T				

In the exam ...

You might be asked to say whether you would prefer to live in a town/city or in the countryside, giving your reasons. You may also be asked to describe the area in which you live, saying why you do or don't like it. You could also be asked to say what could be done to improve the area you live in.

See also: Test 1 Likes and dislikes

Tests 27 and 28 Accommodation

Test 38 The environment

Test 51 Services and facilities

32 Weather

Match the first part of the sentence in the first column with a word in the
second column and the rest of the sentence in the third column. In some
cases, more than one combination may be possible. There is an example at
the beginning (0).

0	A cool, pleasant ...	... mist ...
1	The torrential ...	... smog ...
2	A roaring ...	... wind ...
3	The clatter of ...	... thunderstorm, ...
4	The crashing ...	... lightning ...
5	There was a sudden flash of ...	... clouds ...
6	Thick, grey ...	... breeze ...
7	A thin, grey ...	... snow ...
8	A dirty, yellow ...	... boiling ...
9	I loved the crunch of ...	... sun ...
10	She shook the freezing ...	... rain ...
11	A howling, icy ...	... hurricane ...
12	A blazing ...	... thunder ...
13	A devastating ...	... frost ...
14	Huge, fluffy ...	... blizzard ...
15	Hot, humid air usually precedes a ...	... freezing ...
16	The weather on that summer day was absolutely ...	... fog ...
17	The weather on that winter day was absolutely ...	... hailstones ...

... rolled across the sky and hid the sun.

... echoed across the valley and made everyone jump.

... from her hair as she stepped into the house.

... but after it has broken, the humidity usually drops.

... and everyone decided to stay in out of the cold.

... made it impossible to see more than a few metres ahead of us.

... covered the hills.

... covered the town and made it difficult to breathe.

... hit the window and woke me up.

... underfoot as I walked across the grass.

... shone down on the beach.

... blew gently through the trees and took the edge off the heat.

... turned everything white and made driving conditions very bad.

... and everyone decided to head for the beach.

... destroyed buildings and knocked down trees.

... which lit up the night sky.

... removed the last of the autumn leaves from the trees and turned umbrellas inside out.

... poured down all day and the streets were full of people carrying umbrellas.

33 History and politics

In each of the following sentences, one of the words has been incorrectly used (for example, a noun has been used instead of an adjective, or the wrong form of noun has been used). Identify and correct the word in each case. There is an example at the beginning (0).

0	In <u>prehistory</u> times, my country was a tropical island covered with thick forest.	*prehistoric*
1	The first inhabits arrived from mainland Europe about 10,000 years ago.	_____
2	They built settlers along the rivers and on the coast.	_____
3	About 2,000 years ago, the country was conquering by the Romans.	_____
4	Later on, they were defeat by invading armies from the north.	_____
5	The Romans were forced to departure and so returned home.	_____
6	The country became a king under Homer the First.	_____
7	Most of the kings and queens after him were dictatorships who abused their power.	_____
8	In the sixteenth century, there was a revolting by the poor people.	_____
9	They overthrown the king, who fled the country.	_____
10	A republican was established, but it was very unpopular.	_____
11	After a few years, the country became a monarch again under King Bart.	_____

12 King Bart was also the rule of Lycaenia, and my country became part of his country. _____

13 However, he was unpopular and so the people deposition him in 1892. _____

14 During this time, the country began to become industry. _____

15 Before this, it was mainly an agriculture country. _____

16 My country won its independent from Lycaenia in 1906. _____

17 This was shortly after the Lycaenian governor was assassination. _____

18 During the reign of Queen Marge the First, a democracy system was adopted. _____

19 In 1934, a civilian war resulted in the deaths of thousands of people. _____

20 A republican system was adopted once again, and many agreed that this politician system worked the best. _____

21 In 1936, the first president elections were held. _____

In the exam ...
You are not expected to have in-depth knowledge of the history or political system in your country; the questions in the First Certificate avoid topics which require specialist knowledge. However, you may be asked to describe aspects of your country, and some of the words above may be useful. If *relevant* and *used correctly*, they will certainly impress the examiner!

34 Law and order

Match the sentences on the left with the most suitable response on the right.
Use the words and expressions in **bold** to help you. There is an example at
the beginning (0).

0	Is shoplifting **illegal**?
1	There was a **burglary** last night.
2	There was a **robbery** last night.
3	How can you make sure nobody takes your **valuables** when you are staying in a hotel?
4	I carry a gun so that I can **protect myself**.
5	What's the best way to protect your **property**?
6	What's the best way to prevent **pickpockets** taking your cash when you're travelling?
7	Is your home **well-protected**?
8	He didn't receive any **punishment** at all.
9	He didn't go to **prison**, but the judge decided he had to be punished.
10	How long was he **sentenced** to?
11	What happened after he was **arrested**?
12	Did he **admit** he was **guilty**?
13	Do you have **capital punishment** in your country?
14	Are the police in your country **armed**?
15	The **prison** was very small.
16	The **court** was very busy.
17	When was he **released**?
18	Was the thief **caught**?
19	He killed somebody, but it wasn't intentional, so he wasn't charged with **murder**.

a   Well, make sure you only use it in **self-defence**.

b   Wear a **money belt**.

c   Instead, he was accused of **manslaughter**.

d   There were **lawyers**, **judges** and **police** everywhere.

e   Believe it or not, he was **acquitted**.

f   He received a heavy **fine** instead.

g   He **got out** of jail last week.

h   Put them in a **safe**.

i   No, we no longer **execute** people.

j   The police **charged** him with **robbery** and **shoplifting**.

k   No, he **got away**.

l   Yes. It is **against the law**.

m   No, he said he was **innocent**.

n   **Life** imprisonment.

o   No, but I always **lock** the door and **leave the lights on** when I go out.

p   There were only five **cells**.

q   Fit a **burglar alarm** in the house.

r   Somebody **broke into** the house opposite mine.

s   Somebody **stole** over £20,000 from a bank on the High Street.

t   No, they don't **carry guns**.

35 Education 1

Choose the most appropriate word from A, B, C or D to complete the following sentences 1–13. There is an example at the beginning (0).

0   When I was young, I was sent to _____ school by my parents.

A sleeping   (B) boarding   C staying   D residential

1   In Britain, it is _____ to go to school between the ages of five and sixteen.

A voluntary   B compulsory   C legal   D required

2   Schools which are funded by the government are called _____ schools.

A national   B government   C public   D state

3   Most schools in Britain are called _____ schools, which means they have students with mixed abilities.

A comprehension   B comprehend   C comprehensive
D completion

4   Many children below the age of five go to _____ school.

A nursery   B nursing   C baby   D kindergarten

5   Children between the ages of eleven and sixteen go to _____ school.

A second   B secondary   C secondly   D secretary

6   At school children learn a lot of _____ , such as maths and history.

A objects   B subjects   C topics   D lessons

7   At the age of eighteen, some people _____ university.

A enter   B do   C graduate   D study

8   I got a good grade in my history exam, but unfortunately I _____ my maths.

A passed   B took   C failed   D lost

9   How many times did you _____ your FCE exam?

A study   B make   C pass   D take

10   Unfortunately, Emma didn't _____ her exams.

A succeed   B win   C gain   D pass

11   There wasn't an Italian class at her school, so she _____ herself to speak it.

A learned   B studied   C made   D taught

12   At school, the teacher _____ us about the dangers of drugs.

A learned   B raised   C brought up   D educated

13   I'm _____ German so I can get a job in Munich.

A acquiring   B teaching   C educating   D learning

36 Education 2

Choose the most appropriate word or expression in bold in the following sentences. There is an example at the beginning (0).

0 A young child who goes to school is called a (pupil) / **student**.

1 A class at university is better know as a **lesson / lecture**.

2 Money which is given to a student to help them study is called a **fee / grant**.

3 The people who work at a school or college are called the **crew / staff**.

4 A person who has successfully completed a course at university is called **a graduate / an undergraduate**.

5 A teacher who gives talks to large groups of people at university is called a **tutor / lecturer**.

6 In Britain, the academic year is divided into three **semesters / terms**.

7 Courses in computer studies, retail management and other job training skills are known as **vocational / postgraduate** training courses.

8 You need a lot of **self-discipline / self-control** if you want to succeed at university.

9 Before an exam, you need to **remember / revise** everything for a few weeks.

10   I always used to get terrible **marks / scores** for my geography homework when I was at school.

11   Did you have to wear **a uniform / an outfit** when you went to school?

12   When I go to university, I want to **do / study** for a degree in Information Technology.

13   Don't forget to **do / make** notes during the lesson.

14   I didn't go to German lessons, but I managed to **pick some up / put some by** when I was working in Berlin.

In the exam ...

You might be asked to talk about your school, your favourite subjects or extra-curricular activities at school or your attitudes towards education. You may also have to describe the educational system in your country in a letter, or you may need to describe a school (e.g., its location, facilities, class size etc.) in a report.

37 Language learning

A Match the sentences in the left-hand column with those in the right-hand column, using the words in **bold** to help you. There is an example at the beginning (0).

0	Ben speaks six languages.
1	Raymond speaks two languages.
2	Beth's French is perfect.
3	Sarah's Spanish is adequate for everyday needs.
4	Alan's Greek is really good.
5	I can't understand what he's saying.
6	When Jordi speaks English, he always uses the wrong tenses and puts the words in the wrong order.
7	When you are preparing for your First Certificate exam, you should use an English-English dictionary.
8	Do you know much Japanese?
9	Why did you buy this book?
10	How long have you been studying English?
11	Do you go to English classes?
12	How do you practise your listening skills?
13	What's the best way to remember new words?
14	Did you learn Italian at school?
15	How's your English?
16	How's Mary's Portuguese?
17	You speak English very well.
18	Where does she come from?
19	In my French lessons at school, we just listened to the teacher and repeated everything she said.

a   She speaks it **fluently**.

b   We have a very good **language laboratory** at my school.

c   His **pronunciation** is terrible.

d   In fact, he speaks it **like a native**.

e   I've been **learning** it for five years.

f   No, I'm **teaching myself** from a book.

g   Learning a language **parrot-fashion** isn't very satisfactory.

h   I'm not sure, but from her **accent** I presume she's Japanese.

i   No, I **picked it up** when I was working in Milan.

j   You should **keep a record** of them, and try to **recycle** them as much as possible.

k   He has terrible problems with his **grammar**.

l   I want to improve my **vocabulary**.

m   No, my knowledge is very **limited**.

n   Thanks. Actually, it's my **mother tongue**.

o   He is **bi-lingual**.

p   I'm making **slow progress**.

q   Longman produce good **monolingual** versions.

r   When she goes on holiday, she manages to **get by**.

s   He is **multi-lingual**.

t   She thinks it's **coming along** nicely.

B Which language or languages do people speak in the following countries?

France	_French_	Thailand	_____
Italy	_____	Malaysia	_____
Holland	_____	New Zealand	_____
Canada	_____	Sweden	_____
the USA	_____	Norway	_____
Denmark	_____	Russia	_____
China	_____	Mexico	_____
Switzerland	_____	Turkey	_____
Belgium	_____	Morocco	_____
Saudi Arabia	_____	South Africa	_____
Brazil	_____	Hungary	_____
Japan	_____	Korea	_____
Poland	_____	Singapore	_____
Iran	_____	Indonesia	_____

In the exam ...

You might be asked how long you have been learning English and how you plan to use your English in the future. You may also be asked to say how you feel about language learning – what are the best methods of learning a language, etc.

See also: Tests 35 and 36 Education

38 The environment

Read this article. For each of the numbers 1–21, underline the most appropriate word. There is an example at the beginning (0).

Nowadays, it is difficult to avoid (0) **environment / environmental** issues. We are always being told how (1) **polluted / pollution** is having an adverse effect on our (2) **planet / earth**. (3) **Poisoned / Poisonous** gases from factories destroy the (4) **oxygen / ozone** layer, contributing to the (5) **hothouse / greenhouse** effect which results in global (6) **warming / heating**. (7) **Acidity / Acid** rain is destroying forests. As more and more (8) **rainforest / desert** is destroyed, the threat to (9) **wildlife / wildly life** increases, with several (10) **dangerous / endangered** species already on the verge of (11) **extinct / extinction**. In brief, we are heading towards an (12) **ecological / ecology** disaster.

However, we can all do something to help protect the environment. For a start, we should try to (13) **reserve / conserve** energy (14) **resources / resorts** such as oil and coal, by turning down our central heating or making less use of our cars. Most cars use (15) **leadless / unleaded** petrol, but this still (16) **injures / damages** the environment. Secondly, since many everyday items such as glass and paper can be (17) **recycled / recharged**, we should try to re-use them rather than throwing them away. Thirdly, we can join (18) **pressurising / pressure** groups, which can be very effective in persuading governments to adopt greener (19) **politics / policies**, such as (20) **subsidising / subsiding** public transport and (21) **protecting / defending** wildlife.

In the exam...
Questions on the environment are very common and are often featured in the Reading Paper. In the Speaking Test or Writing Paper you may be asked to give your opinion on the state of the environment and what can be done to save it.
See also: Test 29 Animals and plants

39 Cinema and theatre

Choose the correct words or expressions in **bold** to complete this text. There is an example at the beginning (0).

At the cinema.

Last week I saw an excellent (0) (**film**)/ **performance** at the new cinema on the High Street. It's one of those huge (1) **multi-screen / many-screen** complexes where there is always a (2) **collection / selection** of ten films to choose from.

There was quite a long queue at the box (3) **office / kiosk**, but I got my (4) **ticket / card** (which also included free (5) **admit / admission** to the Museum of Modern Film in London as part of a special (6) **promote / promotion**) and went into the (7) **arena / auditorium**, where the (8) **usher / porter** helped me to find my seat.

The lights went (9) **down / up**, but before the film started we watched some (10) **trailers / previews** for forthcoming films, and some (11) **promotions / advertisements** for soft drinks and fast food restaurants.

The film was a (12) **drama / dramatic** called 'House of the Horse', and is currently on general (13) **release / exhibition** at cinemas across the country. It (14) **stars / shows** actor Brad Gibson in the (15) **role / place** of a man who loses his job and decides to breed racehorses. Gibson gave an excellent (16) **perform / performance**, the (17) **soundtrack / orchestra** was very moving and some of the special (18) **effects / affects** were great. The (19) **audience / spectators** enjoyed it a great deal and although I don't usually like this kind of film – I prefer (20) **thrillers / thrillings**, (21) **horrible / horror** movies and (22) **comedians / comedies**, – I found it very (23) **enjoyable / enjoying**. Unfortunately the newpapers (24) **critics / criticisms** weren't so positive; they thought it was (25) **boring / bored** and generally gave it very negative (26) **reviews / previews**.

At the theatre

The next night I saw a (1) **drama / play** at the Old Rick Theatre in the city centre. It was a (2) **musical / musician** called 'Whistle with Wind' and was (3) **set / located** in a baked-bean factory.

It was a (4) **disaster / disastrous**. The curtain went (5) **on / up** almost half an hour late, and from the beginning it was clear that the whole thing had been very badly (6) **practised / rehearsed**; half the (7) **crew / cast** kept missing their entrances. In the middle of the first (8) **scene / scenery**, there was a power cut, and the entire (9) **stage / platform** was plunged into darkness. At the end of the first (10) **act / action**, half the audience left and at the end of the (11) **performance / performing**, when the curtain finally came (12) **down / up**, the (13) **applause / clap** was very thin. Apparently, the (14) **director / conductor** had resigned a few days before the first night.

I often wonder why people bother paying so much to see (15) **live / alive** shows full of mistakes when they can watch (16) **pre-recorded / ready-made** shows on the television for much less.

In the exam ...
You might be asked to describe a film or a play you have seen recently, and say why you did or didn't enjoy it. You may also be asked to write a report recommending a film, play or other show for other people. You should try to give as much information about it as possible, giving a *brief* description of what it was about, the main characters, aspects that you thought were good or bad, its suitability for different ages and so on.
See also: Test 40 Entertainment

40 Entertainment

Look at the following descriptions of places we go to or things we see during our free time. For each passage, decide what is being described from the box below. <u>Underline</u> the words in each passage that helped you decide. Be careful: there are some things in the box which do not fit in any of the categories. There is an example at the beginning (0).

> a party   an art exhibition   an opera   a television programme
> a̶ ̶n̶i̶g̶h̶t̶ ̶c̶l̶u̶b̶   a ballet   a classical concert   a play
> a radio programme   a football match   a film   a circus
> a restaurant   a funfair or amusement park   a rock concert

0   The floor was packed with people enjoying DJ Catman Morris and his team spinning the latest sounds. Strobe lights flashed as the dancers worked themselves into a frenzy.   _____*a night club*_____

1   As the players walked onto the pitch, the spectators went wild, chanting and singing in support of their favourite team.

_____

2   The audience downstairs in the stalls, and those upstairs in the circle went quiet as the curtain opened to reveal the stage. The lights came up and the cast made their first appearance.

_____

3   This has been a major box office success. The special effects are spectacular and the soundtrack is loud and exciting. The director will probably receive an Oscar for his work, and the main actors have received a lot of praise for their performance. It is currently on general release across the country.   _____

4   The huge auditorium was full to capacity with cheering, singing fans. The lead singer strutted across the stage as his band filled the building with deafening noise.   _____

5   The conductor turned and faced the audience, who were
    enthusiastically applauding the orchestra. The leading musician
    then stepped forward and shook the conductor's hand.

    _____

6   Mimi de Gruchy is an elegant dancer, and as she pirhouetted
    across the stage on the tips of her toes, everybody marvelled at
    her agility.   _____

7   Bernardo Pavlova is a big man with a big voice. His performance
    in Mozart's 'Marriage of Figaro' at the ENO last year won him
    great critical acclaim. He is undoubtedly one of the greatest tenors
    of his time.   _____

8   Good evening viewers, and welcome to a new series of the quiz
    show that promises to make somebody very rich. Here's your host
    for tonight … Chris Smugman!   _____

9   I love watching the clowns and the acrobats, but I can't stand
    watching animals being made to perform. I think it's very cruel.

    _____

10 Hello again listeners, and welcome to today's edition of 'On the
    Air'. In the studio I have with me one of our most famous
    presenters and broadcasters, Bob Jenkins. _____

11 This is a beautiful example of his work. The mix of colours is
    fantastic and I love the way he smears the oils on the canvas.
    What is it? I have no idea!   _____

12 I love the atmosphere of these places: the screams and laughter;
    the hair-raising rides and silly games where you can win a prize;
    the flashing lights and loud music; the smell of popcorn and
    greasy fried food.   _____

41 Media

A Put the words below into their correct box according to the type of media they relate to. In several cases, one word may fit into more than one box. There is an example in each box.

~~website~~ ~~quiz~~ ~~reporter~~ tabloid advertisement
chat show log on ~~author~~ turn on headline domain editor
game show e-mail novel download documentary
paperback weather forecast programme turn off broadcast
broadsheet feature print chapter log off circulation
turn over channel publish commercial hardback
horoscope serial soap opera journalist server
current affairs small ads series sitcom station

Television and radio	Newspapers and magazines
quiz	*reporter*

Books	The internet
author	*website*

B Read these descriptions and decide what is being talked about. You will find the answers in the list on the previous page. In some cases, more than one answer may be possible. There is an example at the beginning (0).

0 This is a good place to consider if you want to buy or sell something. If you want to rent a room or a house, you should look here first. _____*small ads*_____

1 They have a very important job keeping us informed about what is happening around the world. Some of them are very brave, bringing us stories from areas where there is a war or natural disaster. But sometimes they just write rubbish and invade our privacy. _____

2 I prefer these because they have longer, more informative articles and are more serious than the tabloids. Also, they're not full of rubbish! _____

3 They only last for a minute or so, but some of them are actually better than the programmes they interrupt. Some of them are very good at persuading you to go out and buy their products or services. _____

4 It's such a good way to communicate with people. It's much quicker than sending them a letter, and it's cheaper than phoning them, especially if they live a long distance away. _____

5 There are millions of them. Some of them provide you with very valuable information, and it's great to have so much information at your fingertips. Unfortunately, it can sometimes be difficult to find exactly what you want, and if you spend too long accessing them, it can become expensive. _____

6   It's on three times a week, and follows the lives of a group of students who live together. It always ends at an exciting moment and you have to wait for the next episode to find out what happens next. _____

7   Who is my favourite? Probably Graham Greene. His stories were always exciting, and he had such a vivid imagination. A lot of his stories were made into films. _____

8   I watched one last night. It was about Columbus' first voyage to the Americas. It had been well-researched, and the narrator gave lots of interesting information. There's one on tonight about tigers in India that I want to see. _____

9   There are five of these in Britain. Of course, if you have cable or satellite, you can watch hundreds of others from around the world. _____

10   I read mine every day, but I don't really believe in them. I'm an Aries, you see, and we're not very superstitious people.

_____

11   There are over 70 in this book. I'm only on 6!

_____

42 Music

A   Look at the album reviews opposite, and find synonyms from the words in **bold** for the following. There is an example at the beginning (0).

0   The words of a song. ___*lyrics*___

1   A regular sound in a piece of music. _____

2   Directed a piece of music. _____

3   A collection of songs, often by different singers and groups, on one album. _____

4   The parts of a piece of music which are sung. _____

5   Something which you cannot easily forget. _____

6   Person who sings professionally, plays an instrument, writes songs, paints, etc. _____

7   Part of an orchestra comprising the violins, cellos, etc.

_____

8   Extremely loud. _____

9   Somebody who writes and performs their own music. _____

10   Very active. _____

11   An album recorded with an audience present. _____

12   A great or famous piece of music. _____

13   Commercially successful songs. _____

14   Showing emotions of love. _____

15   A musician who plays an instrument on their own, usually as part of a performance supported by a band or orchestra. _____

16   To make music on a musical instrument. _____

17   Soft and rich. _____

18   Person who writes music. _____

19   Modern. _____

a **The Berlin Symphony Orchestra: Longmanius' Violin Concerto No 1**
Helmut Von Karavan was over eighty when he **conducted** this definitive recording by the **contemporary** Swedish **composer**. Violin **soloist** Frederick Klose leads the **string section** with both passion and pathos, and there is excellent back-up from the wind and percussion section.

b **Verona Philharmonic and the Bologna Choral: Mozart's The Marriage of Figaro**
Luciano di Parma is one of the world's finest singers, and his rich barritone voice is heard to best effect on this **live** album. The orchestra, too, are in good form, and help to bring this Mozart **classic** to life. For those of you who want to sing along, the words (together with an English translation) are included inside the album cover.

c **Deathjaw – Scream Dream.**
This album is not for the faint-hearted. Ozzie Gutt's screaming **vocals** and Richie Moreton's **deafening** electric guitar are enough to blow your amplifier. And if *they* don't do it, Bev Powell's thumping drums certainly will! For heaven's sake, don't play this when your grandmother's around!

d **Ricky Rankin' Mann – Caribbean Heat**
If you can't get to Jamaica, then this album is the next best thing. There is an exhilarating **beat** that simply makes you want to find a tropical beach and dance the night away. If you liked Bob Marley, you'll love this.

e **Dizzy Waters – Hot Nights, Cool Sounds**
Nobody can **play** the saxophone like Dizzy Waters, and you only have to listen to this album once to be transported to the steamy, smoke-filled basement clubs of New Orleans. It's smooth and **mellow**. Ideal midnight music for night owls.

f **Various – Can Rave, Will Rave**
This is a **compilation** of the best techno, rave, hip-hop and house music from the last decade. It includes top mixes from the Ibiza scene, and is guaranteed to get everybody on the floor if your party needs livening up.

g **Andy Cheeseman – Champagne and Roses: the best of Andy Cheeseman**
The **singer-songwriter** croons his way through some of his classic love songs. **Sentimental** lyrics and **memorable** tunes will help the evenings pass more quickly. It is the ideal album for incurable romantics everywhere.

h **The Spicy Grills – We Can't Sing**
Profound **lyrics** and **lively** music from one of today's newest groups. This album has already produced three top ten **hits** and looks set to win a number of awards, including best-selling album of the year, best newcomer and most original **artist**. This is essential listening for teenagers everywhere.

B Which of the albums are examples of:

1	reggae	_d_	5	pop	_____
2	jazz	_____	6	dance	_____
3	heavy metal	_____	7	easy listening	_____
4	opera	_____	8	classical music	_____

43 Sport

A The wrong word. Look at these definitions of different things associated with sports, and change the word in **bold** so that it is correct. There is an example at the beginning (0).

0	tea	A group of people who play a sport together.	Add a letter.	*team*
1	reference	A person who supervises games like football.	Remove two letters.	
2	empires	A person who supervises games such as tennis and cricket.	Remove one letter and change another.	
3	opposites	Two or more people playing against each other.	Change four letters.	
4	peach	A field where games like football are played.	Change two letters.	
5	count	A place where games like tennis, squash and volleyball are played.	Change a letter.	
6	coarse	An area of land where golf is played or a race is held.	Change a letter.	
7	snatch	A game of football, tennis, volleyball etc.	Remove one letter and change another.	
8	straining	You wear these when you go running.	Remove one letter and change three others.	
9	help	You wear this on your head for more dangerous sports.	Change one of the letters and add two more.	
10	banter	A wooden instrument used for hitting a ball in games like table tennis and cricket.	Remove three letters	
11	rocket	An instrument used to hit a ball in games like tennis, squash or badminton.	Change a letter.	
12	scout	To gain points in a game or competition.	Change two letters.	

B Choose the most appropriate word to complete the following sentences. There is an example at the beginning (0).

0 If you want to get fit, you should _____ swimming.
A do (B) go C play D make

1 Nobody could have predicted that France would _____ both the 1998 World Cup and the 2000 European Cup.
A succeed B win C gain D beat

2 Which team are you going to _____ in the Cup Final?
A support B encourage C accept D promote

3 When I was young, I wanted to _____ football for England.
A do B make C play D take

4 I _____ jogging to get fit.
A took up B took on C took over D took in

5 If the two teams _____ , there will have to be a re-match.
A even B match C equal D draw

6 If we _____ the game, we'll be out of the competition.
A defeat B lose C fail D withdraw

7 The players will have to _____ hard over the next few weeks in order to win.
A rehearse B train C learn D study

8 We _____ the other team 4:2.
A won B succeeded C beat D conquered

9 Don't forget to _____ plenty of exercise if you want to stay fit.
A make B play C go D take

10 Our team were _____ by two goals to one.
A won B lost C defeated D destroyed

In the exam ...
You might be asked about the sports you play or enjoy watching, and why you like them so much, or you may have to explain how a game is played. You could also be asked to talk about the most popular sports in your country. In the Writing Paper, you might have to write a letter arranging a sports meeting with a school, or describe an exciting event you attended.
See also: Test 44 Free time activities
Test 45 Health and exercise

44 Free time activities

A Match the verbs in X with the items in Y. Some verbs can be used more than once. Here is an example:

We play cards.

X

> play   do   go   collect   make   surf

Y

> cards   rock climbing   the internet   postcards   horse riding
> clothes   hiking   shopping   tennis   photography   camping
> computer games   chess   jogging   cooking   coins
> swimming   skiing   volleyball   antiques   stamps   the piano
> the guitar   things using your hands

B Now look at these following descriptions and decide what is being talked about. <u>Underline</u> the words which helped you to decide. There is an example at the beginning (0).

0 The best time of the day to do this is early in the morning, before it gets too hot. It's not very expensive; all you need is a good pair of <u>trainers</u> and a bit of <u>stamina</u>. It keeps me very fit.

Jogging

1 I spend most of my free time doing this. I love being able to find out so much information by just pressing a button and looking at a screen. It brings the whole world into your house.

2 I go about twice a week. Everybody says that it's the best way of keeping fit. I usually do about fifteen or twenty lengths. If I stay longer, the chlorine really irritates my eyes.

3 Some of them are really exciting, and as technology gets better, they're becoming more realistic. You can do it on your own, or with other people via the World Wide Web.

4   It can be very expensive, since you need to buy things like lenses
     and a flash. The processing and developing can also cost a lot.
     However, it's very satisfying to see the finished product, whether
     it's a slide or a print.   _____

5   I practise every night. As soon as I get home, I plug it into the
     amplifier and turn the volume up. My neighbours must hate me!

                                                           _____

6   I joined the club at my school last year. It's a very peaceful
     activity, but it really makes your brain work, working out moves
     and strategies. It's one of the oldest games in the world.

                                                           _____

7   Most of the time I wander around looking in the windows, but
     sometimes I can't resist going inside and spending something. It
     makes me feel really good. Some people call it retail therapy!

                                                           _____

8   I've got about five hundred from all over the world. I ask my
     friends to send them whenever they go anywhere. My favourite
     one is a picture of Paris in the nineteenth century.

                                                           _____

9   I find chopping and peeling things very therapeutic. And I love
     mixing sauces, marinading meat and fish and so on.
     Unfortunately, I usually manage to burn everything!

                                                           _____

In the exam ...
You may be asked to talk or write about how you like to spend your free
time, or hobbies and activities that you would like to try. You may need to
describe these activities in detail, and explain why you like/would like to do
them. You may also have to describe some activities you did as part of a
holiday, or different hobbies that you have had during different stages of
your life.
See also: Test 43 Sport

45 Health and exercise

Complete the three parts of this story with an appropriate word or expression from the boxes. In some cases, more than one answer is possible. There is an example at the beginning (0).

Part 1

> balanced diet   took up   overweight   give up   cancer
> sedentary   get fit   junk food   look after   diseases
> ~~unhealthy~~   active   heart attacks

My doctor told me I was very (0) __unhealthy__ and that I didn't (1) _____ myself. For a start, I was (2) _____ by about twenty kilogrammes. He said I was a couch potato and needed to change my (3) _____ lifestyle. He also told me about the benefits of leading a more (4) _____ lifestyle. He stressed the importance of sticking to a (5) _____ and insisted that I shouldn't eat so much (6) _____ from fast-food restaurants. In addition, he strongly advised me to (7) _____ smoking. He described to me the horrors of fatal (8) _____ such as (9) _____ and (10) _____. He advised me to (11) _____ and suggested I (12) _____ some exercise.

Part 2

> keep fit   fatty   sports centre   fibre   cut down on   tracksuit
> health club   jogging   trainers   carbohydrates   swimming

Anyway, I bought myself a (13) _____ and a pair of (14) _____. I started going to a (15) _____ where I went (16) _____ and (17) _____. I also started doing some (18) _____ exercises such as aerobics. I then joined a (19) _____ where I had the use of a sauna and got some good advice from a dietitian. I (20) _____

unhealthy foods – those which were (21) _____, such as
meat, or full of (22) _____ and sugar, like cakes and
biscuits – and made sure I consumed more (23) _____.

Part 3

> overdid   broke   shape   slim   twisted   muscles
> weight   cleared up   sprained

To my delight, I lost (24) _____ and became
(25) _____ for the first time in my life. I developed
(26) _____ in places I didn't realize I could develop them.
And my skin problems (27) _____. Unfortunately, one
day I (28) _____ it: I fell off my exercise bike,
(29) _____ my ankle, (30) _____ my wrist and
(31) _____ two ribs!

Somehow, I don't think that two weeks of lying in bed and eating
hospital food will keep me in good (32) _____!

In the exam …
You might be asked to describe different ways of getting fit or staying
healthy. You may have to describe different sorts of exercise that we can
take to get fit, or the sort of food we should and shouldn't eat. In the Writing
Paper, you might have to write a report describing or recommending a
health club or sports centre, or an article recommending a healthier lifestyle.
See also: Test 43 Sport
　　　　　　Test 46 Food

46 Food

How much do you know about food? Answer the questions in this quiz.

0 Which of these words means *to reduce food to small shreds by rubbing it along a rough or sharp surface?*

A chop **Ⓑ** grate   C dice   D slice

---

1 Which of these cooking methods is the healthiest way of preparing food?

A fry   **B** boil   **C** roast   **D** bake   **E** steam   **F** barbecue

---

2 You should always **swallow** food before you **chew** it.

A True   **B** False

---

3 What do we call someone who **doesn't eat meat**? _____

---

4 Which of these words means *to drink slowly?*

A gobble   **B** sip   **C** gulp   **D** slurp

---

5 Choose the correct word in the following sentence.

My mother has a wonderful **receipt / recipe / recite** for roast chicken.

---

6 Eggs, cheese and milk contain a lot of **vitamin C**.

A True   **B** False

---

7 To **eat a balanced diet** and to **go on a diet** have the same meaning.

A True   **B** False

---

8 Rearrange these letters to form a word which gives the name of a substance which is found in food like meat and eggs, and which helps your body to grow and stay healthy: **noprtie** _____

---

9 Foods which are <u>high</u> in **fibre** and <u>low</u> in **fat** are better for you.

A True   B False

10 Which of the following is most important for the development of healthy bones and teeth?

A calcium   B carbohydrates   C cholesterol   D calories

11 What is the difference between the following expressions?

A to **cut down on** something   B to **give** something **up**

_____

_____

12 Complete the following sentences with an appropriate preposition.

I can't eat this meat. It's gone _____.

I don't want to eat at home tonight. Let's eat _____.

I'm fond _____ Mexican food.

She invited me _____ dinner.

I prefer eating at restaurants _____ eating at home.

What are we having _____ lunch?

13 From the list of foods below, choose ones which are: **sweet / salty / hot and spicy / sour / bland or tasteless / bitter / fresh / stale**

A curry _____   E sugar _____

B boiled rice _____   F a packet of peanuts _____

C a new loaf of bread _____   G a lemon _____

D an old loaf of bread _____   H dark chocolate _____

47 Physical appearance

Look at the pictures and read the description of each person. In each picture, there are some mistakes. Circle the words in **bold** which are wrong. There is an example at the beginning (0).

0 My wife Joanne is in her **early thirties**, but she **looks young for her age**. She's **tall** and slightly ~~skinny~~. She has ~~shoulder-length curly hair~~, a ~~turned-up nose~~ and a **generous mouth**.

1 My friend Ron is **short** and a little **overweight**. He is **bald with bushy eyebrows**, and **ears that stick out**. He has **fat cheeks** and a **wrinkled forehead**. He also has a **moustache**. As you can see, he **frowns** a lot and appears to be quite **bad-tempered**.

2 This is my cousin Raymond, who is in his **mid-teens**. He's of **medium height** and has **short, straight, black hair** with a **parting** in the **middle**. There are **freckles** on his face and he has a **hooked nose**. He is quite **dark-skinned**.

3 My mother Rose is in her **mid-forties**. She's about 1.8 metres tall and has **long, blond, wavy hair** with a **fringe** that comes down **over her eyes**. She has a **pale complexion** and a **warm smile**. She is wearing **earrings** and **glasses**.

4 My brother Jasper is very **tall** with **broad shoulders** and **well-developed muscles**. He's 22 years old, but **looks older** because of his **beard**. He has very **short, spiky hair**. When he smiles, he has **dimples** on both cheeks, which makes his **weatherbeaten** face more attractive.

5 This is my sister Amelia. As you can see, she is quite **chubby, with long, black, curly hair**. She has **tanned skin, thin eyebrows** that almost meet in the middle, and **long, thin eyelashes**. She also has a **double chin**, which she's a bit self-conscious of. She always wears a **nose stud** and has a **cheerful smile**.

48 Personal life and experience

Choose the correct word in each sentence. There is an example at the beginning (0).

0   In my (early)/ **low** / **young** thirties I had enough money to buy a house.

1   I **am born** / **was born** / **was being born** in 1965.

2   My parents died when I was a **baby** / **young** / **small**.

3   I was **trained** / **grown up** / **brought up** by my grandmother.

4   My grandmother had to **support** / **prop** / **carry** us with the money she made working in a shop.

5   Of course, we didn't have much money, and lived in terrible **poor** / **poverty** / **poorly**.

6   Naturally, we both dreamed that one day we would live a life of **luxurious** / **luxury** / **luxuriously**.

7   My grandmother always hoped that one day we would be **wealthy** / **wealthily** / **wealth**.

8   As a **children** / **young** / **child**, I didn't fit in with the other kids because I didn't have the things they had.

9   This got worse when I became a **teenager** / **teenage** / **teenaged**.

10   I left school in my **middle teens** / **mid teens** / **central teens**.

11   My grandmother was disappointed that I had decided to **drop into** / **drop down from** / **drop out of** school.

12   Shortly after this, she began to suffer from poor **healthily** / **health** / **healthy**.

13   As a result, she was forced to **retire** / **retirement** / **retired**.

14   With her small pension, we weren't **well on** / **well out** / **well off**.

15   Nevertheless, we managed to **get by** / **get off** / **get out**.

16   Despite our poor circumstances I had **ambitious / ambition / ambiguity** and decided to apply for a good job.

17   For a few months I was **unemployment / unemployed / workless**.

18   I had the **possibility / opportunity / opportune** to go to college, but I didn't have enough money.

19   I **took on / took out / took up** photography as a hobby.

20   I then started **job / work / employ** as an assistant to a photographer.

21   The photographer and I **got together / got on / got out** well and I enjoyed the work.

22   I managed to **put by / put off / put out** a little money, which I kept in the bank.

23   After a few years, I **gave away / gave out / gave up** this job.

24   With the money I had saved, I **started up / started out / started on** my own photographic studio.

25   My venture **did well / made well / did good** and I was able to open another studio.

26   I continued living with my grandmother as she wasn't well enough to live **lone / alone / lonely**.

In the exam ...

You may need to talk or write about your own life and experiences, or those of another person. The information you give doesn't have to be true, although it is usually easier to talk about things that actually happened to you.

When talking or writing about yourself, you may also need to include information about your family and friends, your education, your hobbies and other interests and where you live or come from.

See also: Tests 22 and 23 Friends and relations

               Tests 35 and 36 Education

               Test 44 Free time activities

               Tests 52 and 53 Work

49 Routine

Choose the correct word or expression for each of the following sentences. In many cases, more than one answer may be possible. There is an example at the beginning (0).

0 My alarm clock _____ at six o'clock.

Ⓐ goes off **B** goes out **C** goes up

---

1 Even if I'm fast asleep, it always _____ me _____ .

A makes ... off **B** wakes ... up **C** gets ... up

---

2 Once I'm _____ , I usually lie in bed for a few minutes.

A wake **B** woken **C** awake

---

3 I then _____ .

A get off **B** get up **C** get in

---

4 The first thing I do is _____ a shower.

A make **B** have **C** take

---

5 I _____ my breakfast and have a cup of coffee.

A make **B** do **C** prepare

---

6 Then I _____ my teeth.

A wash **B** clean **C** brush

---

7 After that I _____ .

A put on **B** wear **C** get dressed

---

8   Next, I _____ the children to school.

A fetch   **B** take   **C** bring

9   I walk to the bus stop and _____ the bus to the city centre.

A catch   **B** get   **C** take

10   I work _____ 8 o'clock _____ half past twelve.

A since ... until   **B** from ... to   **C** between ... and

11   After lunch, I _____ a walk in the park.

A take   **B** go for   **C** make

12   At half past three I _____ the children from school.

A pick up   **B** collect   **C** fetch

13   In the evening I like to _____ things _____ .

A make ... easily   **B** take ... easy   **C** go ... slowly

14   Just before I go to bed, I _____ the cat _____ .

A put ... up   **B** put ... aside   **C** put ... out

15   I enjoy _____ in bed before I go to sleep.

A to read   **B** reading   **C** the reading

16   The last thing I do is _____ my alarm clock.

A set   **B** prepare   **C** load

17   I usually _____ at about midnight.

A drop out   **B** drop in   **C** drop off

50 Shopping and consumer goods

Look at the following pairs of sentences. In some cases, the words in **bold** have been used correctly. In other cases, they have been put into the wrong sentence. Decide which are *correct* and which are *wrong*. There is an example at the beginning (0).

0   Some shops offer their customers **debit** if they don't have enough cash. Most people prefer to pay their bills by direct **credit**.

These are both <u>wrong</u>. Shops offer their customers credit, and people pay their bills by direct <u>debit</u>.

1   How much did you **pay** for your new computer.
I don't **spend** much on clothes.

2   In some shops, it's possible to ask for a **bargain**.
The assistant told me the television cost £250. It was such a **discount**!

3   You should check your **change** carefully before you leave the shop.
If you discover that something you have bought is broken, the shop should offer you **an exchange**.

4   I try to avoid shopping on Saturdays, as the streets are full of **shoppers**.
Some shops offer incentives to encourage **customers** to use them.

5   I shop in supermarkets where the **price** of food is low.
Our local florist went out of business because his **costs** were too high.

6   A lot of people go shopping during the **reductions**, when prices are lower.
Our local department store is offering **sales** on all items over £5.

7   There is a street market near our house where there are hundreds of **boutiques** selling cheap food.
I buy my clothes from the very fashionable **stalls** in our local shopping centre.

8   Shops which have a wide range of **goods** attract more customers.
After you've chosen your **purchases**, take them to the cashier to pay.

9   When you pay, make sure you get a **bill**.
The mail order company sent me a **receipt**, which I had to pay within two weeks.

10   The butcher's near my house is **on sale**.
A large range of home computers is **for sale** at the electronics shop on the High Street.

11   The **serve** in our chemist's is terrible.
I had to wait for over ten minutes at the newsagent's before anyone offered to **service** me.

12   Although it's **priced** at £10, you can probably get a 10% discount if you ask.
I think £6 for a hamburger is a bit **pricey**.

13   I buy things in bulk, as it's more **economic**.
Because of **economical** problems, our local off-licence was forced to close.

14   If the shop doesn't have what you want, they can **order** it for you.
Shopkeepers across the country are going to **demand** more police protection from thieves.

15   As prices **come down**, people are no longer able to afford to go shopping.
The customers were delighted when prices started to **go up**.

16   I couldn't buy more floppy disks as the shop was out of **provide**.
We asked if the garage could **stock** us with after-sales service.

17   We needed food for the weekend, so I offered to **do the shopping**.
We were bored, so decided to **go shopping**.

18   I **brought** a new computer at the weekend.
I then **bought** it home and set it up.

Don't forget to use your dictionary to look up the meanings of any words you don't know.

See also: Test 11 Location
Test 51 Services and facilities

51 Services and facilities

What is being described in each case? <u>Underline</u> the words and expressions which helped you to decide. There is an example at the beginning (0).

---

health centre   taxi rank   police station   law courts   bus stop
post office   college   youth hostel   school   health club
town hall   library   hotel   registry office   station
~~restaurant~~   job centre   park   museum

---

0 You'll need to make a <u>reservation</u> a day in advance. The <u>service</u> is excellent and they have a huge range of <u>starters</u>, <u>main courses</u> and <u>desserts</u>.   *restaurant*

1 There are over 20 members of staff and almost 200 pupils. The national syllabus is supplemented by a variety of extra-curricular activities.   _____

2 There is a large variety of materials to borrow, including magazines, journals and audio-visual resources.   _____

3 The platform and waiting room were packed with early-morning commuters, while a long line queued impatiently at the ticket office.   _____

4 We waited in the shelter for the number 7 to take us into town. Eventually, one came along, but the conductor said it was full and we had to wait for the next one.   _____

5 Five doctors work here, helped by a small team of nurses, receptionists and a pharmacist. They can treat minor illnesses, but for more serious problems they will send you to the hospital.

_____

6 The facilities are excellent. There are two gyms, a swimming pool, a sauna and a café serving a variety of nutritious foods.

_____

7 The mayor and town councillors all have offices here. Like most bureaucracies, it's very inefficient.   _____

8 I've been unemployed for almost six months. I go here every week, but so far I've been unable to find work.   _____

9   It's very busy on Sunday afternoons, with couples strolling or sitting on the grass and small children feeding the ducks on the pond or playing on the swings and roundabouts. _____

10 There's a kitchen, lounge and a large dormitory with eighteen beds. Each bed has space underneath for storing your backpack. The wardens are very friendly, but won't allow you to bring your muddy boots into the sleeping area. _____

11 This place is always busy with judges, lawyers, police officers and ordinary members of the public, including defendants, witnesses and jurors. _____

12 This building keeps a record of births, marriages and deaths. You can also get married here if you want a civil wedding. _____

13 In addition to buying stamps and sending mail, you can also pay your electricity, telephone and gas bills, renew your road tax and buy your television licence in this building. _____

14 These places get very busy late at night when everybody is going home. Make sure you stand in line and have enough money for your fare. It's customary to give the driver a tip, too _____

15 There is a large display of artefacts from all over the world and a gallery of fine art. Every weekend there are exhibitions, talks and workshops run by experts. _____

16 There is always a sergeant on duty at the front desk. The officers have their own rooms upstairs. At the back of the building, there are the cells. _____

17 A variety of courses are run here. You can join an evening class if you work during the day. Vocational training is also offered.

    _____

18 Their single, twin and double rooms all have en-suite facilities, mini-bar, satellite television and room service. Many have a balcony. _____

See also: Test 11 Location
Test 31 Town and country

52 Work 1

Complete the following sentences with an appropriate form of the word on the right. There is an example at the beginning (0).

0	John had been ___unemployed___ for almost six months.	**EMPLOY**
1	One day, he saw an _____ in the newspaper for an office job.	**ADVERTISE**
2	He wrote to them and they sent him an _____ form.	**APPLY**
3	There were over 50 _____ for the job.	**APPLY**
4	Unfortunately, he lacked experience and the appropriate _____ .	**QUALIFY**
5	He was _____ and decided to try elsewhere.	**SUCCESS**
6	He was then offered a place on a _____ course offered by another company.	**TRAIN**
7	He completed the course and was able to fill one of the _____ at the company.	**VACANT**
8	As a new _____ , he found it difficult at first.	**EMPLOY**
9	Nevertheless, he was good at his job, and managed to impress his _____ .	**EMPLOY**

10	Within a short space of time, he was _____ .	PROMOTE
11	Unfortunately, he lived a long way from the office and didn't enjoy _____ .	COMMUTE
12	After a while, his _____ dropped as he found the work more demanding.	ATTEND
13	Eventually, the _____ of the company decided to speak to him.	MANAGE
14	He warned John that he would be _____ if he didn't do better.	DISMISS
15	He emphasized that he didn't want to get rid of such an _____ worker.	EXPERIENCE
16	John agreed that he hadn't been doing very well, and offered his _____ .	RESIGN

In the exam ...

You may be asked to describe the types of job you would be interested in for the future (if you are still at school or college), or describe your current job (if you are working). You could be asked to talk about the aspects of your job that you like or dislike, or told to describe your 'ideal' job (where it would be, what you would do, etc.)

53 Work 2

The following sentences all talk about John's experience in the story in the previous test. For each sentence, choose the most appropriate word. There is an example at the beginning (0).

0 When John saw the job advertised, he wrote to the **personal** / (**personnel**) manager.

1 He was interested in the **post** / **part** that was being offered.

2 He needed to provide the names of two **referees** / **referrals** who would tell his potential employer what he was like.

3 At the **interrogation** / **interview**, he was unsuccessful.

4 He met the other **candidates** / **applications**.

5 The course he followed offered **vocational** / **skilful** training.

6 He **earned** / **won** a good **pay** / **salary** for his job.

7 The company offered him a **retirement** / **pension** scheme.

8 He received a pay **raise** / **rise**.

9 He received good **perks** / **promotions**, such as free healthcare, free lunches at work and a company car.

10 He had good **aspects** / **prospects** for the future.

11 His boss threatened to **resign** / **sack** him if he didn't work harder.

12 He didn't get much job **satisfy** / **satisfaction**.

13 Other workers in his company were made **redundant** / **redundancy** when the company had financial problems.

14 He sometimes had to work **overtime / extra time** on busy days.

15 He had to pay a lot of **income / salary** tax.

16 He **gave up / gave away** his job because he couldn't handle the pressure.

17 He found another job, and remained with that company for the rest of his working life before **resigning / retiring** at the age of 65.

54 Picture description

Cover up the pictures opposite and read the following description. Try to remember as much as possible. Then cover this page and look at the pictures. Decide which one is being described.

I'm looking at a picture of a tropical beach. I can see a couple of people, one of them leaning against a palm tree which is on the left of the picture. There's a creature – I think it's a lizard – climbing up the tree, and in the bottom right-hand corner I can see something which looks like a crab. In the foreground there's a boat and, behind the boat in the middle-distance there seem to be some dolphins playing in the water. In the middle distance, roughly in the middle of the picture, there's a small island. In the far distance, on the horizon, there's a ship moving towards the left of the picture. In the top left-hand corner there's an aeroplane and to the right of the aeroplane, there's a flock of birds, probably seagulls. It looks very peaceful and relaxing.

In the exam ...

You will need to talk about two photos in the Speaking Test. Your description does not have to be in too much detail, but you should describe briefly what you can see and what you think is happening. Expressions such as *I think it's...*, *It looks like...*, *There seem(s) to be ...* and *It's probably...* are quite useful to remember.

55 Interview expressions

Here are some expressions that you may find useful in the Speaking Test. Put each expression into the correct box. There are eight expressions that would not be appropriate. There is an example in each box.

1	I'm afraid I don't agree with you.	17	Could you repeat that, please?
2	I'm sorry?	18	Shut up and let me speak.
3	That's rubbish!	19	In other words …
4	What do you think about …?	20	I don't entirely agree with you.
5	Don't just sit there like a stuffed cabbage.	21	What are your feelings about …
6	Let me see.	22	Pardon?
7	Yes, I agree.	23	I'm not so sure about that.
8	What I mean is …	24	Eh?
9	What's your opinion?	25	How can I put this?
10	I'm afraid I didn't catch that.	26	Would you mind repeating that?
11	What?	27	What are your views on …
12	That's exactly my view.	28	That's absolute nonsense.
13	Put a sock in it.	29	Get lost.
14	That's just what I was thinking.	30	Can I think about that for a moment?
15	To put it another way …	31	What I'm trying to say is …
16	I couldn't agree more.		

Asking somebody what they think	Asking somebody to clarify or repeat something
What do you think about ...?	*I'm sorry?*

Agreeing with somebody	Disagreeing with somebody
Yes, I agree.	*I'm afraid I don't agree with you.*

Giving yourself time to think	Saying something in another way
Let me see.	*What I mean is ...*

56 Writing a letter

Look at these two letters. One of them is formal, the other is informal. In each letter, choose the word or expression that is most appropriate to the register of the letter. In a few cases, it may be possible to use either. There is an example in each letter (0).

An informal letter

Dear Marcus

(0) **Thank you very much** / Thanks a lot for your postcard. (1) **It was great to hear from you again / I very much appreciated your early reply**, and I'm really looking forward to seeing you in Paris next week. Anyway, (2) **as you requested / you asked me about** my (3) **plans / itinerary** for the trip, and here they are.

I will (4) **depart / leave** Heathrow Airport at about nine o'clock and should arrive in Paris at about ten o'clock. At quarter past one I will (5) **go to / attend** the student conference at the International Centre. This (6) **commences / begins** at about half past one, stops for tea at four and then (7) **recommences / starts again** at five (I have been (8) **told / informed** there is a restaurant (9) **on the premises / there**, so I won't go hungry!). The whole thing ends at about seven, when I'll go to check into my hotel.

(10) **I regret / I'm sorry** that I (11) **am unable to / can't** meet you as soon as I arrive, but (12) **do you fancy meeting / would you like to meet** me later, at about half past eight? (13) **Why don't we meet / I suggest meeting** at the *Belle Vache* restaurant on the Boulevard Beaumarchais, which is (14) **handy / convenient** for my hotel. (15) **It would be great / I would be grateful** if you could let me know what you think.

I hope (16) **that's everything / I have covered the main points**. If you (17) **require / need** any (18) **more / further** information, feel free to (19) **contact me / give me a call** on my mobile.

Please (20) **give my kindest regards / give my love** to Nadine and Odile.

(21) **Keep in touch / I look forward to hearing from you soon.**

(22) **Yours sincerely / Best wishes**

Robert

A formal letter

Dear Mr Pearson

(0) ~~Thank you very much~~ / Thanks a lot for your letter of 23 February.
(1) **It was great to hear from you again / I very much appreciated your early reply**. (2) As **you requested / you asked me about**, here is the (3) **plans / itinerary** for my trip to France next week.

9.00   (4) **Depart / Leave** London-Heathrow on BA flight 264

10.15   Arrive Paris-Orly

1.15   (5) **Go to / Attend** student conference at the International Centre. This (6) **commences / begins** at about 1.30, breaks for tea at 4.00 and then (7) **recommences / starts again** at 5.

7.30   Meeting ends. Check into Campanile Hotel at Place de la Bastille.

(8) **I regret / I'm sorry** that I (9) **am unable to / can't** meet you until the following day, as I have an important meeting in the evening. (10) **I suggest meeting / Why don't we meet** at your office, as this would be (11) **handy / convenient** for all of us. Or (12) **do you fancy meeting / would you like to meet** me at the International Centre? I have been (13) **told / informed** that they have private meeting room facilities (14) **on the premises / there** which we could use.

I hope (15) **that's everything / I have covered the main points**. If you (16) **require / need** any (17) **more / further** information, please do not hesitate to (18) **contact me / give me a call** at the above address. In the meantime, (19) **I would be grateful / it would be great** if you would call me to confirm the location for our meeting.

Please (20) **give my kindest regards / give my love** to Mrs Langsdale.

(21) **Keep in touch / I look forward to hearing from you soon**.

(22) **Yours sincerely / Best wishes**

Robert Watkins

Robert Watkins

In the exam ...

Although modern business letters tend to be less formal than they used to be, the First Certificate examiners like to see that you are able to distinguish between formal and informal styles, so it is quite useful to learn the various words and expressions needed for both. Remember that in formal letters, you should not use idiomatic, colloquial or slang words and expressions. You should not use contractions (for example, *I'm* instead of *I am*). If you begin your letter *Dear Sir / Madam*, you should finish with *Yours faithfully*).

57 Writing a story

Complete the story below, using the expressions from the box. In some cases, there is more than one possible answer. There is an example at the beginning (0).

> I was horrified to discover   to my horror   as a result   luckily
> it was then   at first   until   when   it wasn't until   suddenly
> a few years ago   in desperation   after a while   that I discovered
> to my disappointment   then   to my surprise   in relief

(0) *A few years ago* I lost my job (1) _____ my company closed down. Fortunately, I had saved a bit of money, so was able to get by (2) _____ I could find another job.

(3) _____, the money began to run out, and (4) _____ I still hadn't found a job. (5) _____, I decided to take drastic action; I decided to rob a bank!

(6) _____, everything was very simple. I drove to the Great West bank in Bristol and parked my car outside. (7) _____ I walked into the bank, approached a cashier and demanded £5,000. (8) _____, she gave me the cash without any argument. (9) _____, an alarm started ringing. I ran out of the bank, relieved to have been so successful. (10) _____ I was standing on the pavement that I realised something had gone horribly wrong. (11) _____ somebody had stolen my car!

(12) _____, I decided to stop the first vehicle that came along. I ran into the road, waving my arms at an approaching car. (13) _____ it stopped, and I jumped into the back seat.

'Quick! Get me out of here!' I shouted at the driver. He accelerated away from the bank and I sat back (14) _____.

(15) _____, when the driver and his passenger turned to face me, (16) _____ what a terrible mistake I had made. (17) _____, the car I had stopped was a police car!

58 Writing a report

A student has been asked by her teacher to recommend an English school in Britain which would be suitable for an exchange programme.
Look at the report she wrote and choose the correct words or expressions in bold which are most suitable. There is an example at the beginning (0).

(0) **I would like to recommend** / Why don't we go to St. Blodwyn's, a large school in Oxford. I visited the school last month and was shown what it has to offer. (1) **I was pleased to see / To my amazement**, it offers everything that we need.

(2) **First of all / At first**, the school is located in a peaceful residential district of North Oxford, within easy reach of the city centre, so it would be (3) **very simple / dead easy** for our students to visit the university colleges, museums and galleries in this (4) **really old / historic city**.

(5) **And then / Secondly**, the school has a reputation for (6) **high quality / absolutely brilliant** teaching, with (7) **tiny / small** classes of no more than twelve students. The teachers themselves (8) **are all fully-qualified / know their stuff**, with (9) **loads of / a great deal of** experience. The school caters for students of all levels. (10) **However, / What a pity** the minimum age is 16, and this will prevent some of our younger students from attending.

(11) **In addition to / Despite** the teaching, the school has (12) **excellent / smashing** facilities, including a computer room and a self-access centre (13) **equipped / stuffed** with a large variety of books and other learning (14) **resources / things**. A restaurant and snack bar provide students with (15) **delicious / yummy** food throughout the day.

(16) **Furthermore / What's more**, the accommodation is very (17) **comfortable / cosy**. Most of the rooms have en-suite facilities, and each accommodation block has a variety of recreational facilities such as darts and snooker, which are (18) **great fun / perfect** for relaxing in the evenings.

The school runs an active social programme, with a selection of activities, but I (19) **don't know / haven't got a clue** if these are included in the price of the courses. I will (20) **write to the school / drop the school a line** to find out.

(21) **In my opinion / If you ask me**, for the above reasons, St. Blodwyn's would be (22) **ideal / brilliant** for our forthcoming exchange programme. I'm sure (23) **you'd absolutely love it / you will agree it is the ideal choice for our purposes**.

59 Writing a composition or article

For the following sentences, choose the most appropriate word or expression in **bold**. There is an example at the beginning (0).

0 (Despite)/ **Although** the changeable weather, Britain is a very pleasant country to visit.

1 **Despite** / **Although** it rains a lot, it never gets very cold.

2 Learning English in an English-speaking country can be very rewarding. **Furthermore** / **Nevertheless**, it can be very difficult to adjust to a new way of life.

3 English is spoken as a first language in a lot of countries. **Furthermore** / **Nevertheless**, it is also the language of international communication.

4 London is a very busy city, **whereas** / **however** towns like Oxford and Cambridge are slightly more relaxed.

5 The pressures of living in a big city can be very demanding. **Whereas** / **However**, city life does have its rewards.

6 **In my opinion** / **According to me**, the more languages you speak, the better your future prospects.

7 I **believe that** / **consider** travel makes you more aware of the world around you.

8 Many people **consider** / **believe that** the internet to be the most important invention since the wheel.

9 On one **side** / **hand**, developments in information technology are changing our lives. On the other **side** / **hand**, they are moving too quickly for us to keep up.

10   It is certainly true that the environment is in trouble. **First of all / In the beginning**, pollution is making the air almost unbreathable in big cities. **Next / Secondly,** industrial pollution causes global warming, which is affecting the polar ice caps. **Moreover / Then** destruction of the rainforests is destroying wildlife.

11   The air in cities is often very dirty, **in contrast / while** the air in the country is usually fresh and clean.

12   The weather in Spain is often warm and sunny. **While / In contrast**, England is often cold and damp.

13   **As well as / In addition** learning grammar, you should also try to develop your vocabulary.

14   Grammar is very important. **As well as / In addition**, you should try to develop your vocabulary.

15   **In addition to / In addition** recording new words and expressions that you learn in your lessons, you should recycle them whenever possible.

16   **In the end / In conclusion**, I would like to say that everyone should try to learn English in an English-speaking environment.

17   There are many things you can do to improve your English, but **in the end / in conclusion** there is no substitute for taking a course in an English-speaking country.

In the exam ...

The words and expressions above are all useful if you have to write a composition or article in the exam. You should try to use a variety of these to express your opinion or link ideas.

See also: Test 58 Writing a report

60 Writing about a set text

In most of the lines of this book review, there is a mistake. Sometimes the wrong word has been used, and sometimes the wrong <u>form</u> of the word has been used. If there are no mistakes, put a tick in the grid. If there is a mistake, identify it and write the correct word in the grid. There are two examples at the beginning (0) and (00)

0	I would like to tell you about 'Rebecca', a (storybook) which was
00	written in the 1930s by the English author Daphne du Maurier.
1	It is both a love story and a mysterious, full of action, romance,
2	intrigue and atmosphere.
3	There are five main actors in the story: the narrator, whose
4	name we never discovery; Max de Winter, a wealthy middle-
5	aged man; Mrs. Danvers, his sinisterly housekeeper; Max's
6	first wife, Rebecca, a beautiful but arrogant woman who makes an
7	important play in the story, even though she is dead, and Jack
8	Favell, Rebecca's cousin and a selfishly playboy.
9	The story is placed in Monte Carlo, and later at 'Manderley', Max's
10	estate in the west of England, where most of the acting takes
11	place. The narrator, a young woman, explains how she meets
12	Max in Monte Carlo, falls in love and marries him. They
13	return to England, where they move to Max's house. Whereas, the
14	narrator is not happily, because the house is full of memories of
15	the death Rebecca. Mrs. Danvers, who adored Rebecca, treats
16	the narrator very badly, and Max remains cold and distant.
17	The narrator then uncovers that Max murdered Rebecca
18	because she was having affairs with other men. Although this

19 she still loves him, and promising to help him. However, Jack

20 Favell finds out what Max has done and threatens him with

21 blackmail. The story ends very drama, with Mrs. Danvers

22 burning 'Manderley' to the ground, and Jack Favell promising to

23 get revenge to Max.

24 In my concern, 'Rebecca' is one of the best books I have ever

25 read, and I would advise it to anyone.

0	_novel_	8	___	17	___
00	✔	9	___	18	___
1	___	10	___	19	___
2	___	11	___	20	___
3	___	12	___	21	___
4	___	13	___	22	___
5	___	14	___	23	___
6	___	15	___	24	___
7	___	16	___	25	___

In the exam ...

The questions on the set text do not usually ask you to write a straightforward description of the story, as above. Instead you will probably be asked to focus on a particular aspect of the text (location, characters, important events, how the story ends, etc.) and comment on this.

Answers

Section 1: General vocabulary

Test 1
Likes
1 fancy	5 long for
2 adore	6 attracted to
3 worship	7 fond of
4 look forward to	8 keen on

Dislikes
1 hate	5 can't bear
2 loathe	6 repels
3 detest	7 disgust
4 can't stand	8 revolt

Test 2
A

Things we do with our arms and hands:

beckon	crawl	cross	flex
grab	grope	nudge	pat
point	punch	rub	slap
snap	squeeze	stretch	stroke
tap	throw	wave	wipe

Things we do with our mouth and nose:

cough	groan	hiccup	laugh
mutter	pant	puff	scream
shout	sigh	snarl	sneeze
sniff	snore	stammer	whisper
yawn	yell		

Things we do with our feet and legs:

crawl	creep	cross	dash
jump	leap	limp	march
slip	stagger	stretch	stroll
tap	trip	trudge	wander

Things we do with our eyes:

blink	frown	gaze	glance
glare	glimpse	peep	peer
stare	watch	wink	

B
1 crawled	8 frowning
2 screamed	9 waving
3 trudging	10 snored
4 glimpsed	11 tapping
5 beckoning	12 glared
6 sneezed	13 nudged
7 creep	14 sighed

Here are some other words which you might find useful.

bend	climb	crouch	doze
faint	fall	fidget	lean
nod	pull	push	salute
smile	sob	shake	shiver
shrug	skip	squat	sweat
tremble			

Test 3
1 A	2 C	3 B	4 C	5 A
6 C	7 B	8 B	9 A	10 C
11 B	12 A			

Test 4
1 now	13 damage
2 affects	14 job
3 yet	15 kind
4 afraid of	16 lend
5 prevented	17 lay
6 fetch	18 countryside
7 chance	19 worthless
8 continual	20 rise
9 wonderful	21 remind
10 fun	22 view
11 go	23 sensitive
12 go with	24 bring

Test 5
1 making, doing	10 took, made
2 make, took	11 do, make
3 done, do	12 took, done
4 Take, made	13 take, do
5 take	14 made, took
6 made, take	15 do, make
7 took, made	16 made, doing
8 take, make	
9 Taking *or* Doing, doing	

Test 6
1 achieve	11 fetch
2 become	12 have
3 understand	13 manage
4 buy	14 finish
5 start/leave	15 leave
6 annoys	16 succeed
7 reach	17 depresses (me)
8 prepare	18 enter
9 earn	19 meet
10 persuade	

Test 7
1 T	2 F	3 F	4 T	5 F	6 F
7 F	8 T	9 F	10 T	11 F	12 F
13 F	14 T	15 T	16 F	17 T	18 T

Test 8
1 astonishment
2 death
3 developments
4 disappearance
5 discovery
6 loss
7 permission
8 behaviour
9 laughter
10 embarrassment
11 pleasure
12 signature
13 complaint
14 announcement
15 pronunciation (not pronounciation)
16 success
17 arrival
18 performance
19 argument (not arguement)
20 happiness (not happyness)
21 violence
22 heat
23 patience
24 similarities
25 sympathy
26 confidence
27 probability
28 height

Test 9
1 attractive	16 active
2 industrial	17 changeable
3 additional	18 apologetic
4 residential	19 suspicious
5 beautiful	20 satisfying
6 reasonable	21 bored (not
7 ambitious	boring)
8 wealthy	22 comparative
9 lonely	23 recognisable
10 amusing	24 competitive
11 beneficial	25 creative
12 enjoyable	26 preferable
13 effective	27 doubtful
14 dangerous	28 dependable
15 financial	29 disappointing

Test 10
1 F	2 G	3 K
4 B	5 C	6 I

Test 11
A The underground station
B Walton Square
C Peach Street
D Supersave supermarket
E The florist
F Mr. Greasy's fast food restaurant
G Club Latino
H Thatcher Avenue
I The police station
J The sports shop
K Searle Street
L Pogle Park
M Nibbles café
N Gruchy Lane
O Harridge's department store
P The library
Q **The English school**
R The hospital

Test 12
1 adjust	11 promote
2 alter	12 reduce
3 cure	13 renew
4 demote	14 renovate
5 disappear	15 replace
6 dissolve	16 swell
7 exchange	17 switch
8 expand	18 transform
9 fade	19 vary
10 increase	

Test 13
1 unbelievable	25 unfashionable
2 disobedient	26 unwelcome
3 inadequate	27 misbehave
4 dishonest	28 mistrust
5 unacceptable	*or* distrust
6 imperfect	29 unwrap
7 irregular	30 discontinue
8 irresponsible	31 unfold
9 unlimited	32 impersonal
10 uneven	33 incomplete
11 dislike	34 inaccurate
12 misunderstand	35 illegal
13 mispronounce	36 disagreeable
14 unlock	37 impossible
15 disconnect	38 immature
16 unqualified	39 dissatisfied
17 unavoidable	40 illogical
18 incompetent	41 uncomfortable
19 unconscious	42 disagree
20 uncertain	43 disobey
21 unattractive	44 disapprove
22 impatient	45 unpack
23 unfair	46 uncover
24 unmarried	47 disappear

Test 14

1 save/put by/put aside	11 hit
2 leaves/departs	12 punish
3 filled	13 forgot
4 borrowed	14 receive
5 crying	15 built
6 forbids/bans	16 won
7 denied	17 refused
8 set	18 defend
9 failed	19 working
10 failed	

Test 15

1 false/artificial/fake	13 light
2 stale	14 guilty
3 recorded	15 late
4 soft	16 absent
5 blunt	17 lazy
6 pale/light	18 voluntary
7 loose	19 calm
8 tough	20 wide (not
9 public	*short*)
10 bright	21 generous/kind
11 shallow	22 minor
12 permanent	23 weak

Test 16

1 against	5 at	9 on
2 of	6 in	10 with
3 among	7 during	11 into
4 for	8 to	12 about

Test 17

1 b	2 i	3 l	4 j	5 g
6 h	7 e	8 a	9 n	10 k
11 c	12 d	13 m		

Test 18

1 By the time/When
2 Once/When
3 formerly
4 earlier/previously
5 While/When
6 when
7 Throughout/During
8 In the meantime/Meanwhile
9 Following
10 As soon as/When
11 Over/During
12 Back in
13 ever since
14 from now on

Section 2: Topic vocabulary

Test 19

1 put on	7 match
2 wear	8 grown out of
3 fit	9 out
4 try them on	10 do up
5 ironed	11 supermodel
6 suits	12 change

Test 20

1 A	2 C	3 B	4 B	5 C
6 C	7 B	8 A		

Test 21

1 G	2 D	3 A	4 E	5 H
6 F	7 C	8 B		

Test 22

A
A Tony	G Stanley
B Claudia	H Sue
C Stuart	I Bob
D Claire	J Maureen
E Sally	K John
F Andrew	L Emma

B *Positive feelings:* Emma, Maureen, Sally, Andrew, Claudia, Sue, Claire
Negative feelings: John, Bob, Tony, Stanley, Stuart

Test 23

1 an acquaintance
2 my colleague
3 my fiancée
4 my ex-girlfriend
5 my steady girlfriend
6 my classmate
7 my workmate
8 my flatmate
9 a good friend
10 just good friends

Test 24

1 brochures	12 gate
2 book	13 board
3 tickets	14 cabin crew
4 passport	15 safety belt
5 currency	16 takes off
6 cheques	17 lands
7 suitcase	18 customs
8 check in	19 sunbathing
9 boarding card	20 sightseeing
10 departure lounge	21 check out
11 duty free	

Test 25

1 B	2 A	3 C	4 B	5 C
6 A	7 D	8 C	9 D	10 B
11 B				

Test 26

1 package holiday
2 camping holiday
3 cruise
4 skiing holiday
5 safari
6 hiking holiday
7 sailing holiday
8 sightseeing holiday
9 all-inclusive holiday

Test 27

1 castle	6 country cottage
2 terraced house	7 villa
3 detached house	8 bungalow
4 mansion	9 caravan
5 flat	

These words have a positive connotation:
cosy   spacious   bright
airy   homely   roomy   practical
These words have a negative connotation:
damp   draughty   cramped
pretentious   depressing   seedy
squalid   basic
claustrophobic   pokey

Test 28

A A study	I bathroom
B cellar	J bedroom
C living room	K utility room
D garden	L kitchen-diner
E terrace	M path
F hall	N porch
G shed	O front door
H bedsit	P stairs

B 1 evict	4 decorate
2 demolish	5 lease
3 mortgage	

Test 29

A *Pets/domestic animals:* tortoise, rabbit, hamster, puppy, kitten, white mouse, parrot
Farm animals: horse, duck, cow, sheep, goat, pig
Birds: penguin, duck, eagle, pigeon, parrot
Endangered species: orang-utan, rhinoceros, whale, tiger, panda, dolphin

Reptiles: tortoise, snake, crocodile, lizard, alligator
Insects and invertebrates: cockroach, spider, bee, butterfly, ant
Fish and other water creatures: octopus, whale, shark, trout, lobster, dolphin
Flowers: orchid, daisy, tulip, rose, daffodil
Trees and other plants: oak, chestnut, palm, cactus, bamboo

B 1 penguin	10 tortoise
2 tiger	11 horse
3 whale	12 trout
4 palm	13 butterfly
5 puppy	14 sheep
6 rose	15 duck
7 kitten	16 cactus
8 oak	17 panda
9 snake	

Test 30

1 continents	11 forest/rainforest
2 islands	12 valley
3 D	13 Equator
4 ranges	14 volcano
5 B	15 hurricane/typhoon/
6 deserts	cyclone/storm
7 oceans	16 earthquake
8 waterfalls	17 C
9 canals	18 the North Pole
10 Lake	19 a small river
	20 C

Test 31

1 rural	12 crowded
2 amenity	13 peaceful
3 commuter	14 safe
4 rush hour	15 cosmopolitan
5 green belt	16 field
6 suburb	17 agriculture
7 pollution	18 estate
8 nightlife	19 skyscraper
9 congestion	20 block
10 nature	21 industry
11 stressful	

Test 32

1 ...rain...poured down all day...
2 ...wind / hurricane...
removed the last of the autumn leaves....
destroyed buildings.../...
3 hailstones...hit the window...

4 ...thunder... echoed across the valley...
5 ...lightning...which lit up the night sky
6 ...fog...made it impossible to see... / ...covered the hills
7 ...mist... covered the hills
8 ...smog...covered the town... / made it impossible to see...
9 ...frost / snow...underfoot as I walked....
10 ...snow... from her hair as she...
11 ...blizzard...turned everything white
12 ...sun...shone down on the beach.
13 ...hurricane...destroyed buildings...
14 ...clouds ...rolled across the sky...
15 ...thunderstorm...but after it has broken...
16 ...boiling...and everyone decided to head...
17 ...freezing...and everyone decided to stay...

Test 33
1 inhabits = inhabitants
2 settlers = settlements
3 conquering = conquered
4 defeat = defeated
5 departure = depart
6 king = kingdom
7 dictatorships = dictators
8 revolting = revolution/revolt
9 overthrown = overthrew
10 republican = republic
11 monarch = monarchy
12 rule = ruler
13 deposition = deposed
14 industry = industrialised
15 agriculture = agricultural
16 independent = independence
17 assassination = assassinated
18 democracy = democratic
19 civilian = civil
20 politician = political
21 president = presidential

Test 34
The most suitable responses are:

1 r	2 s	3 h	4 a	5 q
6 b	7 o	8 e	9 f	10 n
11 j	12 m	13 i	14 t	15 p
16 d	17 g	18 k	19 c	

Test 35

1B	2D	3C	4A	5B
6B	7A	8C	9D	10D
11D	12D	13D		

Test 36
1 lecture	8 self-discipline
2 grant	9 revise
3 staff	10 marks
4 graduate	11 uniform
5 lecturer	12 study
6 terms	13 make
7 vocational	14 pick some up

Test 37
A

1 o	2 a	3 r	4 d
5 c or k	6 k	7 q	8 m
9 l	10 e	11 f	12 b
13 j	14 i	15 p	16 t
17 n	18 h	19 g	

B France = French
Italy = Italian
Holland = Dutch
Canada = English/French
the USA = (mainly) American English
Denmark = Danish
China = Chinese (but there are lots of different **dialects**)
Switzerland = French/German/Italian
Belgium = French/Flemish
Saudi Arabia = Arabic
Brazil = (mainly) Portuguese
Japan = Japanese
Poland = Polish
Iran = Farsi
Thailand = Thai
Malaysia = Malay and also Chinese dialects and Indian languages
New Zealand = English
Sweden = Swedish
Norway = Norwegian
Russia = (mainly) Russian
Mexico = Spanish
Turkey = Turkish
Morocco = (mainly) Arabic/French
South Africa = (mainly) English/Afrikaans
Hungary = Hungarian
Korea = Korean
Singapore = English, Malay, various Chinese dialects, various Indian languages
Indonesia = Indonesian

Test 38

1 pollution	12 ecological
2 planet	13 conserve
3 Poisonous	14 resources
4 ozone	15 unleaded
5 greenhouse	16 damages
6 warming	17 recycled
7 Acid	18 pressure
8 rainforest	19 policies
9 wildlife	20 subsidising
10 endangered	21 protecting
11 extinction	

Test 39

At the cinema

1 multi-screen	14 stars
2 selection	15 role
3 office	16 performance
4 ticket	17 soundtrack
5 admission	18 effects
6 promotion	19 audience
7 auditorium	20 thrillers
8 usher	21 horror
9 down	22 comedies
10 trailers	23 enjoyable
11 advertisements	24 critics
12 drama	25 boring
13 release	26 reviews

At the theatre

1 play	9 stage
2 musical	10 act
3 set	11 performance
4 disaster	12 down
5 up	13 applause
6 rehearsed	14 director
7 cast	15 live
8 scene	16 pre-recorded

Test 40

1 a football match
2 a play
3 a film
4 a rock concert
5 a classical concert
6 a ballet
7 an opera
8 a television programme
9 a circus
10 a radio programme
11 an art exhibition
12 a funfair or an amusement park

Test 41

A *Television and radio:* quiz, reporter, chat show, turn on, headline, game show, documentary, weather forecast, programme, turn off, broadcast, turn over, channel, commercial, serial, soap opera, current affairs, series, sitcom, station
Newspapers and magazines: quiz, reporter, tabloid, advertisement, headline, editor, weather forecast, broadsheet, feature, print, circulation, horoscope, journalist, current affairs, small ads
Books: author, editor, novel, paperback, print, chapter, publish, hardback
The internet: website, log on, domain, e-mail, download, log off, server

B		
1 reporters	7 author
2 broadsheets	8 documentary
3 commercials	9 channels
4 e-mail	10 horoscope
5 websites	11 chapters
6 soap opera	

Test 42

A		
1 beat	12 classic
2 conducted	13 hits
3 compilation	14 sentimental
4 vocals	15 soloist
5 memorable	16 play
6 artist	17 mellow
7 string section	18 composer
8 deafening	19 contemporary
9 singer-songwriter	
10 lively	
11 live (pronunciation = /laɪv/)	

B	1 d	2 e	3 c	4 b
	5 h	6 f	7 g	8 a

Test 43

A		
1 referee	7 match
2 umpire	8 trainers
3 opponents	9 helmet
4 pitch	10 bat
5 court	11 racket
6 course	12 score

B	1 B	2 A	3 C	4 A	5 D
	6 B	7 B	8 C	9 D	10 C

Test 44

A *Play:* cards, tennis, computer games, chess, volleyball, the piano, the guitar

Do: photography, cooking, things using your hands
Go: rock climbing, horse riding, hiking, shopping, camping, jogging, swimming, skiing
Collect: postcards, coins, antiques, stamps
Make: clothes, things using your hands
Surf: the internet

B
1 the internet	6 chess
2 swimming	7 shopping
3 computer games	8 postcards
4 photography	9 cooking
5 the guitar	

Test 45
Part 1
1 look after
2 overweight
3 sedentary
4 active
5 balanced diet
6 junk food
7 give up
8 diseases
9/10 hearts attacks/cancer (in either order)
11 get fit
12 took up
Part 2
13 tracksuit
14 trainers
15 sports centre
16/17 jogging/swimming (in either order)
18 keep fit
19 health club
20 cut down on
21 fatty
22 carbohydrates
23 fibre
Part 3
24 weight
25 slim
26 muscles
27 cleared up
28 overdid
29/30 twisted/sprained (in either order)
31 broke
32 shape

Test 46
1 E
2 False – you should always chew it before you swallow it.
3 a vegetarian
4 B
5 recipe
6 False. Vitamin C is found in fruit and vegetables.
7 False. *To eat a balanced diet* is to eat the right amount of food from the different food groups. *To go on a diet* is to eat less in order to lose weight.
8 protein
9 True
10 A
11 *To cut down on something* means to eat less of a certain kind of food. *To give something up* means to stop eating a certain kind of food altogether
12 off/out/of/to;for/to/for
13 curry = hot and spicy; boiled rice = bland or tasteless; a new loaf of bread = fresh; an old loaf of bread = stale; sugar = sweet; a packet of peanuts = salty; a lemon = sour; dark chocolate = bitter

Test 47
1 Ron is not bald, he has a smooth forehead, a beard, not a moustache, and he has a cheerful expression.
2 Raymond has curly hair, not straight hair, and the parting is at the side, not in the middle. He is fair-skinned, not dark-skinned. He doesn't have a hooked nose or any freckles.
3 Rose doesn't have a fringe and she isn't wearing any glasses. She is dark-skinned with dark hair, instead of having a pale complexion and blond hair, and she isn't smiling. In fact, she looks quite severe.
4 Jasper does not have broad shoulders or well-developed muscles. In fact, he is quite skinny. He has a moustache, not a beard, his hair is curly, not spiky and he doesn't have a particularly weather beaten face.
5 Amelia does not have tanned skin, she is quite pale. She doesn't have a double chin or a stud in her nose. She has short, spiky hair, not long, black, curly hair.

Test 48

1 was born	14 well off
2 baby	15 get by
3 brought up	16 ambition
4 support	17 unemployed
5 poverty	18 opportunity
6 luxury	19 took up
7 wealthy	20 work
8 child	21 got on
9 teenager	22 put by
10 mid teens	23 gave up
11 drop out of	24 started up
12 health	25 did well
13 retire	26 alone

Test 49

1 B	10 B and C
2 C	11 A and B
3 B	12 A, B and C
4 B and C	13 B
5 A and C	14 C
6 B and C	15 B
7 C	16 A
8 B	17 C
9 A, B and C	

Test 50

1 correct	7 wrong	13 wrong
2 wrong	8 correct	14 correct
3 correct	9 wrong	15 wrong
4 correct	10 wrong	16 wrong
5 correct	11 wrong	17 correct
6 wrong	12 correct	18 wrong

Test 51

1 school	10 youth hostel
2 library	11 law courts
3 station	12 registry office
4 bus stop	13 post office
5 health centre	14 taxi rank
6 health club	15 museum
7 town hall	16 police station
8 job centre	17 college
9 park	18 hotel

Test 52

1 advertisement	9 employer(s)
2 application	10 promoted
3 applicants	11 commuting
4 qualifications	12 attendance
5 unsuccessful	13 manager
6 training	14 dismissed
7 vacancies	15 experienced
8 employee	16 resignation

Test 53

1 post	10 prospects
2 referees	11 sack
3 interview	12 satisfaction
4 candidates	13 redundant
5 vocational	14 overtime
6 earned/salary	15 income
7 pension	16 gave up
8 rise	17 retiring
9 perks	

Section 3: Exam tasks

Test 54

Picture 4

Test 55

Asking somebody what they think: 4, 9, 21, 27

Asking somebody to clarify or repeat something: 2, 10, 17, 22, 26

Agreeing with somebody: 7, 12, 14, 16

Disagreeing with somebody: 1, 20, 23

Giving yourself time to think: 6, 25, 30

Saying something in another way: 8, 15, 19, 31

3, 5, 11, 13, 18, 24, 28 and 29 are all inappropriate

Test 56

Informal letter
1 It was great to hear from you again
2 you asked me about

3 plans	7 starts again
4 leave	8 told
5 go to	9 there
6 begins	10 I'm sorry

11 can't
12 do you fancy meeting
13 Why don't we meet
14 handy
15 It would be great
16 that's everything

17 need	20 give my love
18 more	21 Keep in touch
19 give me a call	22 Best wishes

Formal letter
1 I very much appreciated
2 As you requested
3 itinerary
4 Depart
5 Attend
6 commences (*begins* is also good)

7 recommences (*starts again* is also good)
8 I regret
9 am unable to
10 I suggest meeting
11 convenient
12 would you like to meet
13 informed (*told* is also good)
14 on the premises (*there* is also good)
15 I have covered the main points
16 require (*need* is also good)
17 further (*more* is also good)
18 contact me
19 I would be grateful
20 give my kindest regards
21 I look forward to hearing from you soon
22 Yours sincerely

Test 57
1 when
2 until
3 After a while
4 to my disappointment
5 As a result / In desperation
6 At first
7 Then
8 To my surprise/Luckily
9 Suddenly
10 It wasn't until
11 I was horrified to discover/To my horror
12 In desperation
13 Luckily/To my surprise
14 in relief
15 It was then
16 that I discovered
17 To my horror / I was horrified to discover

Test 58
1 I was pleased to see
2 First of all
3 very simple
4 historic
5 Secondly
6 high quality
7 small
8 are all fully-qualified
9 a great deal of
10 However
11 In addition to
12 excellent

13 equipped
14 resources
15 delicious
16 Furthermore
17 comfortable
18 perfect
19 don't know
20 write to the school
21 In my opinion
22 ideal
23 you will agree it is the ideal choice for our purposes

Test 59
1 Although
2 Nevertheless
3 Furthermore (we can also say 'What's more')
4 whereas
5 However
6 In my opinion
7 believe that
8 consider
9 hand
10 First of all/ Secondly/ Moreover
11 while
12 In contrast
13 As well as
14 In addition
15 In addition to
16 In conclusion
17 in the end

Test 60
1 mysterious = mystery
2 ✓
3 actors = characters
4 discovery = discover
5 sinisterly = sinister
6 makes = has / plays
7 play = part/role
8 selfishly = selfish
9 placed = set
10 acting = action
11 ✓
12 ✓
13 Whereas = However/Unfortunately
14 happily = happy
15 death = dead
16 ✓
17 uncovers = discovers
18 Although = Despite
19 promising = promises
20 ✓
21 drama = dramatically
22 ✓
23 to = on
24 concern = opinion/view
25 advise = recommend